Quarto is the authority on a wide range of topics.

Quarto educates, entertains and enriches the lives of
our readers—enthusiasts and lovers of hands-on living.

www.quartoknows.com

Publisher: Maxime Boucknooghe
Editorial Director: Victoria Garrard
Art Director: Miranda Snow
Project editor: Sophie Hallam
Design and Editorial: Cloud King Creative
Consultant: Pete Robinson
CSciTeach of the Association for Science Education

First published in the UK by QED Publishing
Part of the Quarto Group, The Old Brewery, 6 Blundell Street, London, N7 9BH

A catalogue record for this book is available from the British Library.

ISBN 978 1 78493 598 6

Printed in China

88½ SCIENCE EXPERIMENTS

NICK ARNOLD

CONTENTS

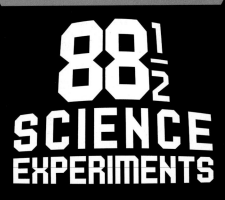

88 ½ SCIENCE EXPERIMENTS

AIR EXPERIMENTS

MIXTURE EXPERIMENTS

WATER EXPERIMENTS

ENERGY & SOUND EXPERIMENTS

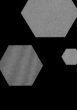

FORCE
EXPERIMENTS

ELECTRICITY & MAGNETISM
EXPERIMENTS

LIGHT
EXPERIMENTS

BODY
EXPERIMENTS

NATURE
EXPERIMENTS

MYSTERY EXPERIMENT

THE THREE RULES OF EXPERIMENTING

RULE #1

BE ORGANIZED

Before you start the experiment, read the WHAT YOU NEED list of materials and equipment. Make sure you have everything you need. If you go off in search of something halfway through an experiment, it may not be safe and it might ruin your results. If you can't find what you need, feel free to use a similar item, but ALWAYS ask before you borrow anything!

All great scientists know the three golden rules of experimenting. These rules show you how to experiment safely and happily.

RULE #2

BE SAFE

This is a book for safe scientists. Adult supervision is always needed with experiments. Pay attention to all the DANGER warnings. In particular, NEVER drink or eat an experiment unless this book says you can.

- BEWARE of hot water.
- BEWARE of climbing on anything and falling off.
- BEWARE of harmful bugs or insects when trying some experiments.

This book doesn't need electricity, fire, or harmful chemicals—so don't use them in your experiments!

BE CLEAN

Take care not to spill messy materials like water or food colouring. Always clean up before you start a new experiment. Cleaning up sounds seriously boring, but it helps you. Yes, really! Cleaning up...

- Clears space for your next experiment.
- Keeps you from losing vital equipment.
- Keeps younger kids from playing with your experiments and hurting themselves or breaking your equipment.
- Means you won't get grounded and banned from experimenting!

WHAT'S NEXT?

Look out for the "What's Next?" challenge. Search for clues to explore and develop the experiments in the book – and find the answers for yourselves! See if you can set up your own lab area at home, with a box for your lab equipment. You could keep a notebook with the results of your experiments.

AIR EXPERIMENTS

1

Air is amazing stuff, and our first set of experiments will show you just how incredible it really is!

THE GREAT COASTER RACE

The way things fall – and the speed in which things fall – has everything to do with air.

WHAT YOU DO

1 Place the coaster on the paper and draw around it.

2 Carefully cut out the shape of the coaster.

3 Hold the coaster between the finger and thumb of one hand. Hold the paper cutout in the same way with your other hand. Stand on a chair and drop them both from a height of 1.5 metres (you will need an adult to help you). What do you notice?

4 Now place the paper cutout over the coaster and drop them both from 1.5 metres.

WHAT HAPPENS?

QUIZ QUESTION:

WHAT WILL HAPPEN AT STEP 4?

A) THE PAPER CUTOUT FALLS FASTER WITH THE COASTER

B) THE PAPER CUTOUT FLIES UPWARDS

C) THE COASTER FALLS SLOWER WITH THE PAPER CUTOUT

ANSWER: A

For a simple experiment, there's a surprising amount of science. **Gravity** pulls on any object. As an object falls, air pushes back. This is called **air resistance**.

Air resistance tries to slow the object's fall. Objects with greater **density** fall faster because they push harder through the air. There is less air resistance with light paper, so it falls more slowly. Now, for Step 4, the air flowing around the paper cutout keeps it close to the coaster. This adds extra weight to the paper cutout, which helps it to fall faster.

WHAT YOU NEED

Coaster (at least 10 cm across)

Scissors

Pencil

Tape measure

Paper

Chair

STAND WITH YOUR ARMS 1.5 METRES FROM THE GROUND FOR STEPS 3 AND 4

DID YOU KNOW?

If you dropped a feather and a 1 kg weight on the Moon, they would fall at the same speed. Earth's air makes the feather fall slower, but there's no air on the Moon.

WHAT'S NEXT?

Try Step 4 with the paper cutout under the coaster. What happens and why?

UPSIDE-DOWN GLASS TEST

*This **air pressure** experiment sets powerful forces against each other. Try the experiment over a sink in case the wrong force wins!*

WHAT YOU NEED

A square of flexible plastic e.g soft CD sleeve

Small glass

Twice as wide as the glass

WHAT YOU DO

1 Fill the glass halfway with water.

2 Wet the square of plastic and the glass rim. Firmly press the plastic over the glass.

3 Holding the plastic in place, gently turn the glass upside down over a sink.

4 Remove your hand from the plastic.

QUIZ QUESTION:

WHY DOES THE PLASTIC STAY IN PLACE?

A) THE PLASTIC IS NATURALLY STICKY WHEN IT'S WET

B) THE FORCES KEEPING THE PLASTIC IN PLACE ARE STRONGER THAN THE FORCES TRYING TO DISLODGE IT

C) GRAVITY DOESN'T WORK WHEN THE GLASS IS UPSIDE-DOWN

WHAT HAPPENS?

ANSWER: B

Gravity tries to make the square of plastic and water fall, but air pressure outside the glass pushes up to keep the plastic in place.

The plastic is also held by water **molecules** pulling on other water molecules to make a skin of water. This is called **surface tension**.

SURFACE TENSION

MAKE A TROMBONE

Ever heard the wind whistling? Don't wait for a windy day – it's easy to make your own musical wind instrument!

WHAT YOU NEED

Bottle

Drinking straw (shorter than the bottle)

WHAT YOU DO

1. Fill the bottle with water, leaving 3 cm at the top.

2. Place the drinking straw in the bottle.

3. Blow across the top of the straw while moving it up and down.

QUIZ QUESTION:

WHICH IS CORRECT?

A) THE HIGHER THE STRAW, THE HIGHER THE SOUND

B) THE HIGHER THE STRAW, THE LOWER THE SOUND

C) THE STRAW CARRIES ON WHISTLING AFTER I STOP BLOWING

WHAT HAPPENS?

ANSWER: B

The straw contains a column of air. Blowing across the straw makes the air vibrate, and the vibrations are what make the sound.

DID YOU KNOW?

When the straw is held higher, the column of air is longer. This creates a deeper sound. A real trombone works pretty much the same way.

The longest time anyone has ever played one note on a wind instrument is one minute and 13 seconds. Can you beat that?

CRAZY COLA

Fizzy drinks are bad for you, but they reveal an amazing, bubbly secret....

WHAT YOU NEED

Glass

Can of cola

Brand-new empty spray bottle

WHAT YOU DO

1 Wash the spray bottle with soapy water. Fill with water.

2 Open the cola and pour it into a glass.

3 Wait for the cola to stop bubbling and then spray it with water.

4 Do not drink the cola—pour it all away!

QUIZ QUESTION:

WHAT WILL HAPPEN TO THE COLA?

A) IT FIZZES UP

B) IT MAKES A LOUD BURPING NOISE

C) IT GLOWS IN THE DARK

ANSWER: A

To make a fizzy drink, carbon dioxide is forced into the drink under pressure. Fizzy drinks contain **dissolved** carbon dioxide gas.

WHAT HAPPENS?

The spray pushes air into the cola, forms bubbles, and the dissolved carbon dioxide gas enters the bubbles. The bubbles get bigger, then rise and pop with a fizzing sound.

WARNING!

ONLY USE A BRAND-NEW AND EMPTY SPRAY BOTTLE. OTHERS MAY CONTAIN HARMFUL CHEMICALS.

WHAT'S NEXT?

Try the same experiment with flat (non-fizzyy) cola. Does it still work—if not, why?

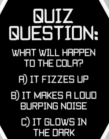

THE BALLOON-EATING BOTTLE

Air presses on objects with a force called air pressure. This experiment shows air pressure in action....

WHAT YOU NEED

Small balloon

Large glass bottle

Ice cubes

Scissors

2 bowls big enough for bottle

WHAT YOU DO

WARNING! ASK AN ADULT WHEN USING HOT WATER

1 Cut 2 cm off the neck of the balloon.

2 Fill the bowl with cold water, add a few ice cubes, and leave it in the fridge for two hours.

3 Fill the bottle with hot tap water and leave for 60 seconds.

4 Fill the sink with hot water. Empty the bottle into the spare bowl, then quickly roll the balloon neck over the top of the bottle. Place the bottle in the sink and watch what happens.

5 Then stand the bottle up in the bowl of cold water.

WHAT HAPPENS?

QUIZ QUESTION:

WHAT WILL HAPPEN TO THE BALLOON?

A) IT TURNS RED AT STEP 4

B) THE BALLOON IS SUCKED INTO THE BOTTLE AT STEP 4 AND SWELLS AT STEP 5

C) IT SWELLS AT STEP 4 AND IS SUCKED INTO THE BOTTLE AT STEP 5

WHAT'S NEXT?

Place the bottle and balloon in a bowl of warm water. What happens?

AIR PRESSURE

ANSWER: C

Air consists of gas molecules, mostly nitrogen and oxygen. Trapped in the bottle, the molecules move around and crash into the balloon sides, creating air pressure. Air pressure increases with temperature, inflating the balloon.

As air in the bottle heats up, the air molecules move faster and need more space – the air expands. This makes the balloon inflate slightly.

When the bottle is in cold water, the air cools down and contracts (shrinks). Air pressure on the outside pushes the balloon into the bottle.

SINK A CORK

You can sink a cork using the power of air!

WHAT YOU NEED

Cork

Bowl of water

Glass

WHAT YOU DO

1 Float the cork in the bowl of water.

2 Slowly place the glass over the cork.

3 Push the glass down with your finger.

QUIZ QUESTION:

WHAT WILL HAPPEN TO THE CORK?

A) THE CORK SINKS, BUT THE WATER LEVEL STAYS THE SAME

B) THE CORK RISES AND THE WATER SINKS

C) THE WATER RISES AND THE CORK SINKS

WHAT HAPPENS?

ANSWER: C

The air in the glass cannot escape or compress easily. The air in the bowl pushes the water up, and the cork sinks because it is now floating on the water in the glass.

WHAT'S NEXT?

Tip the glass sideways to let some air out. What happens to the water level? Why is this?

WATER RISES ➔

CORK SINKS ➔

MAKE AN AIR ROCKET

Air can sink a cork, but can it also make a rocket fly?

WHAT YOU NEED

Sticky tape

Empty 2-litre plastic bottle with cap removed

A4 paper

Scissors

WHAT YOU DO

1. Fold the A4 paper into fourths, unfold, then cut off one quarter using the folded lines as a guide.

2. Roll the quarter paper lengthways from one corner to make a cone. Leave a hole about 0.5 cm wide at the end of the cone. Secure the cone with sticky tape.

3. Place the cone over the bottle and put it on a smooth, hard floor. Hold out both hands. Clap your hands together hard on the bottle's sides.

HOLE

TAPE

QUIZ QUESTION:

WHY DOES THE CONE FLY?

A) THE CLAPPING FORCES AIR OUT OF THE BOTTLE. THIS REDUCES AIR RESISTANCE SO THE CONE CAN FLY

B) AIR FROM THE BOTTLE IS FORCED INTO THE CONE, BOOSTING AIR PRESSURE

C) CLAPPING HEATS AIR IN THE BOTTLE AND LIFTS THE CONE

ANSWER: B

Forcing air into the cone boosts air pressure, especially towards the top. So the cone flies.

WHAT HAPPENS?

DID YOU KNOW?

Real air-powered water rockets can fly hundreds of metres into the air.

15

CRUSH A BOTTLE

You may not actually notice it, but air constantly presses on your body with great force.

WHAT YOU DO

1. Put on the gloves and place ice cubes in the plastic bag.

2. Take the bag outside and crush the ice cubes on a hard surface using the rolling pin. Make sure the ice pieces are small enough to pass through the funnel.

3. Place the bottle in the sink. Using the funnel, quickly pour the crushed ice into the bottle.

4. Place the bottle top back on and turn the bottle sideways. Shake it hard for a few seconds.

WHAT YOU NEED

- 500-ml plastic bottle with top
- Plastic food bag
- Funnel
- 300g of ice cubes
- Gloves
- Mallet or rolling pin

QUIZ QUESTION:

WHAT WILL HAPPEN TO THE BOTTLE?

A) THE BOTTLE SWELLS UP

B) THE ICE INSTANTLY MELTS

C) THE BOTTLE GETS CRUSHED

WHAT HAPPENS?

ANSWER: C

Cold air has lower air pressure. Ice cools air in the bottle and lowers its air pressure. The bottle is squashed by the higher air pressure outside it.

WHAT'S NEXT?

Imagine trying this experiment on the Moon, where there is no air. There would be no pressure outside trying to squash the bottle. The air inside the bottle would probably blow it apart!

WARNING!

ICE CAN BURN YOUR SKIN. DON'T TOUCH IT WITHOUT GLOVES.

WEAKER AIR PRESSURE

STRONGER AIR PRESSURE

WHAT A BLOW!

You might think that you're very strong, but are you stronger than air?

WHAT YOU NEED

Empty 2-litre plastic bottle

Paper tissue

AIR EXPERIMENTS

WHAT YOU DO

1 Scrunch the tissue into a ball. The ball should be small enough to fit in the neck of the bottle and large enough to be a tight fit.

2 Now try to blow the tissue ball into the bottle.

WARNING!
DON'T BREATHE IN – YOU DON'T WANT TO SWALLOW THE TISSUE!

QUIZ QUESTION:

WHAT WILL HAPPEN?

A) EASY– I BLEW THE BALL INTO THE BOTTLE WITH NO TROUBLE

B) I TRIED UNTIL I WAS RED IN THE FACE, BUT I COULDN'T SHIFT THE BALL

C) THE BOTTLE SHOT OUT OF MY MOUTH AND HIT THE CAT!

WHAT HAPPENS?

ANSWER: B

The bottle is full of air with no way out. This air pushes back on the ball just as hard as you can blow. The ball won't move and you'll eventually get tired.

PUT YOUR MOUTH HERE AND BLOW

DID YOU KNOW?

As you compress air, you give it some energy. The energy makes the air molecules move faster, and that makes the air hotter. This explains why a bicycle pump tube heats up when you pump up a tyre.

AIR EXPERIMENTS

MAGIC BOTTLE

It looks like a magic trick, but it's not. It's a daring double act featuring air pressure and surface tension!

WHAT YOU DO

1. Make 5 or 6 holes in the bottle's base using the drawing pin.

2. Fill the bottle with water over a sink and replace the top.

3. Now loosen the top of the bottle.

AIR

QUIZ QUESTION:

WHAT WILL HAPPEN?

A) WATER COMES OUT OF THE HOLES AT STEPS 2 AND 3

B) NO WATER COMES OUT AT ALL

C) WATER ONLY COMES OUT AT STEP 3

WHAT HAPPENS?

ANSWER: C

Surface tension stops water from leaving the holes at Step 2.

When you let air into the bottle, increased air pressure overcomes the surface tension and pushes water through the holes.

DID YOU KNOW?

Liquids in space form floating balls. The liquids are weightless, so gravity can't distort their shape.

WHAT'S NEXT?

Dip a ballpoint pen into a glass of water until a drop forms at its tip when you remove it. You may need a magnifying glass to see the drop clearly. Can you see how surface tension pulls the drop into a ball of water? Give it a shake and see how it changes as it falls.

WHAT YOU NEED

Drawing pin

500-ml plastic bottle with cap

Pen

Magnifying glass

Glass of water

AIR QUIZ

MATCH THE WORDS TO THE ITEMS:

1) NO AIR   2) CARBON DIOXIDE   3) AIR RESISTANCE

A Fizzy drink   **B** Moon   **C** Parachute

Answers: 1) B, 2) A, 3) C.

This liquid is transparent, tasteless, and you can't live without it. Water is one of the most essential elements on the planet... and it's fun to experiment with too!

BLOW A BUBBLE INSIDE A BUBBLE

Did you know that bubbles are actually a lot tougher than they look? Welcome to the watery science of bubbles!

WHAT YOU DO

1 To make the bubble mixture, add 1 teaspoon of water to 7 teaspoons of washing-up liquid in the glass. Cool the mixture in the fridge for two hours.

2 Make the blower by cutting 4 vertical slots 2.5 cm long in one end of the first straw. Then bend the sides out as shown.

3 Wet the bottom of the plastic cup and turn it upside down. Dip the blower in the bubble mixture and blow a large bubble. Gently place the bubble on the upturned bottom of the plastic cup.

4 Wet the second plastic straw and dip it in the bubble mixture. Gently push the straw through the wall of the bubble, and softly blow a smaller bubble.

WARNING!
ASK PERMISSION FROM AN ADULT BEFORE TRYING THIS EXPERIMENT – IT'S MESSY!

QUIZ QUESTION:
HOW CAN YOU PUSH A STRAW INTO A BUBBLE WITHOUT POPPING IT?
A) THE BUBBLE SKIN IS TOUGHER THAN IT LOOKS
B) THE WET STRAW FORMS PART OF THE BUBBLE
C) THE AIR IN THE STRAW STRENGTHENS THE BUBBLE

WHAT HAPPENS?

ANSWER: B
When the wet straw pushes through the bubble, the liquid on the straw becomes part of the bubble wall. As long as you're very gentle, you won't burst it.

The wall of a bubble is made of a very thin layer of water sandwiched by detergent. Detergent molecules reduce surface tension so the bubble can form.

WHAT YOU NEED

Plastic cup

Glass

Washing-up liquid

Scissors

2 plastic drinking straws

Teaspoon

STRAW

2.5 CM

DID YOU KNOW?

If you blew a bubble at -25°C it would turn into an instant ice bubble and fall to the ground.

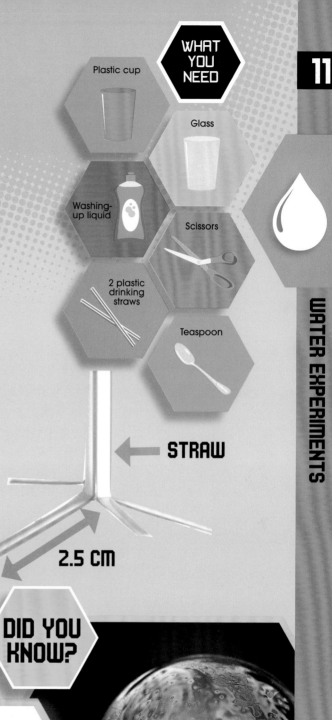

WHAT'S NEXT?

What happens when your inner bubble touches the wall of the outer bubble? Can you blow two bubbles inside one large bubble?

EGG SUBMARINE

Do you think it's possible to turn an egg into a submarine? Let's try it and see!

WHAT YOU DO

1 Draw a submarine on the egg. Gently add the egg to half a glass of warm water. What happens?

2 Now remove the egg and add 5 tablespoons of salt. Stir to dissolve the salt.

3 Replace the egg.

4 Use the jug to trickle warm water down the sides of the glass until it's full.

WHAT YOU NEED

Egg

Large glass

Permanent marker

Jug of warm water

Salt

Tablespoon

QUIZ QUESTION:

WHERE WILL THE EGG END UP AT STEP 4?

A) FLOATING IN THE MIDDLE OF THE GLASS

B) FLOATING ON TOP OF THE WATER

C) SUNK TO THE BOTTOM

WHAT HAPPENS?

ANSWER: A

Objects sink if their density is greater than the density of the water. This is why the egg sinks at Step 1.

Salt increases the density of water, so the egg floats at Step 3.

DID YOU KNOW?

The fresh water floats on the denser salty water. The egg is denser than the fresh water but not as dense as the salty water, so it floats in the middle.

LESS DENSE WATER

DENSE EGG SINKS

A submarine dives by filling its tanks with water. This increases the density of the sub, so it sinks. It surfaces by emptying its tanks.

CONTROL A CORK

A cork bobs about randomly. But this science experiment reveals a way to control it without even touching it!

WHAT YOU NEED

Jug of warm water

Glass

Cork and knife

Washing-up liquid

WHAT YOU DO

1 Ask an adult to cut a slice of cork less than 1 cm thick.

2 Fill the glass three-quarters full of cold water, and then place the cork in the water.

3 Very slowly fill the glass using the jug of warm water. Continue until the water is about to overflow.

QUIZ QUESTION:

WHAT WILL HAPPEN AT STEP 3?

A) THE CORK MOVES AROUND IN CIRCLES

B) THE CORK BOBS UP AND DOWN

C) THE CORK SLOWLY MOVES TOWARDS THE CENTRE OF THE GLASS

WHAT HAPPENS?

ANSWER: C

Surface tension tries to stop the water from overflowing. The water bulges into a gentle dome. The cork floats to the highest point – the centre.

WHAT'S NEXT?

Reduce the surface tension with a few drops of washing-up liquid. What happens to the cork now, and why?

MOVE A COIN

Water is strong stuff. See what happens when you try to push a coin on it!

WHAT YOU NEED

A smooth surface such as a table

Small, light coin

Glass of water

WHAT YOU DO

1 Place the coin on the table and flick it so it shoots across the smooth surface.

2 Pour a little water on the surface of the table.

3 Place the coin on top of the water and then push the coin again.

QUIZ QUESTION:

WHAT WILL HAPPEN TO THE COIN?

A) IT WAS HARDER TO MOVE THE COIN AT STEP 3

B) IT WAS EASIER TO MOVE THE COIN AT STEP 3

C) THE COIN FLIPS ON ITS SIDE AND STARTS ROLLING

WHAT HAPPENS?

ANSWER: A

Surface tension helps water molecules cling together, and this makes water a little sticky. The water around the coin is also quite dense. This is why it's harder to push the coin through water than air.

WHAT'S NEXT?

Imagine running and then swimming. Why is swimming 50 metres more tiring than running that distance?

FLICK COIN

SURFACE TENSION

FLOAT A PIN

WHAT YOU NEED

Washing-up liquid

Clear bowl of warm water

Pin

Drinking straw

Surface tension is surprisingly strong, but can it be beaten by a pin?

WHAT YOU DO

1 Carefully place the pin in the water.

2 Add washing-up liquid to the water one drop at a time.

3 Gently stir the washing-up liquid with a straw to disperse it across the surface of the water.

QUIZ QUESTION:

WHAT WILL HAPPEN TO THE PIN?

A) ONE END OF THE PIN STICKS OUT OF THE WATER

B) THE PIN SLOWLY SINKS

C) THE PIN TURNS BLACK

WHAT HAPPENS?

ANSWER: B

At Step 1, surface tension causes the pin to float. As you add washing-up liquid, it starts to sink.

Washing-up liquid contains detergent. When you add this at Step 2, detergent molecules stop water molecules from clinging together so tightly, reducing surface tension, so the pin sinks.

DID YOU KNOW?

Detergent molecules pull on greasy fat molecules and help to remove them from dirty dishes.

SURFACE TENSION CAUSES THE PIN TO FLOAT

WATER EXPERIMENTS

WATER RACES

Gravity makes water fall down, but water can actually climb, too. You'll believe it once you've tried this experiment ....

WHAT YOU DO

1 Cut a strip of greaseproof paper 2 cm wide and as long as the bowl is deep.

2 Roll the greaseproof paper a few times around the spoon handle and secure with modelling clay. Set up the experiment as shown below. Pour water into the bowl until the strip hangs 1 cm below the surface.

3 Leave the experiment for 2 minutes. Pick up the spoon and mark with a pen how far the water has soaked up the greaseproof paper.

4 Repeat Steps 1, 2 and 3 with newspaper, kitchen towel and writing paper. Make sure the paper strips are all the same length.

WHAT YOU NEED

Wooden spoon

Modelling clay

Newspaper, greaseproof paper, kitchen towel and writing paper

Pen

Bowl

Stopwatch

Scissors

QUIZ QUESTION:

WHICH PAPER WILL SOAK UP THE MOST WATER?

A) SOFTER PAPER

B) HARDER PAPER

C) THEY'RE ABOUT THE SAME

WHAT HAPPENS?

ANSWER: A

Paper is made of **cellulose fibres** and air gaps. Water molecules stick to the cellulose and pull other water molecules up behind them.

Surface tension allows water to bulge upwards into the air gaps. Soft paper soaks up more water because it has more air gaps.

DID YOU KNOW?

Plant stems contain cellulose. Water travels up the stems to the leaves in much the same way as your experiment.

CHILL OUT!

This great experiment demonstrates what happens when you freeze and heat up water molecules.

WHAT YOU NEED

2 identical mugs

Ice cubes

Microwave

WHAT YOU DO

1 Fill one mug two-thirds full with ice and place it in the freezer for 90 minutes.

2 Fill the other mug two-thirds full with cold water from the tap.

3 Ask an adult helper to place both mugs in the microwave and set the timer for one minute.

WARNING!
DO NOT PLACE METAL OR PLASTIC IN A MICROWAVE. DO NOT MICROWAVE FOR MORE THAN ONE MINUTE.

QUIZ QUESTION:
WHAT WILL HAPPEN TO THE WATER IN EACH MUG?

A) THE WATER IS WARM AND THE ICE HAS MELTED

B) THE WATER IS WARM AND THE ICE HASN'T MELTED

C) THE ICE TURNS A WEIRD SHADE OF BLUE

WHAT HAPPENS?

Water molecules are drawn together by surface tension. When water freezes, the molecules lock in place.

It takes a lot of energy to pull the water molecules apart in ice. The energy from the microwave shakes the molecules, but most of the ice stays frozen.

ANSWER: B

Microwaves zap water molecules to and fro – this is what we feel as heat. But ice is solid water.

DID YOU KNOW?

Microwaves are a form of **radiation** like light or radio waves. They vibrate in just the right way to shake water molecules and warm them up.

MOVE A DRINK

Here's a way to move liquids without getting your hands soaking wet!

WHAT YOU DO

1. Place two straws end-to-end and tape them together. Add the other straws to make one long straw.

2. Fill the jug with water and place it on a table.

3. Bend the connected straws as shown. Place one end of the straw in the jug.

4. Using your mouth, suck some water up from the other end of the straw. Place that end in the glass and hold it below the level of the table. Wait and see what happens.

WHAT YOU NEED

Large glass

Large jug

4 bendy straws

Wide sticky tape

Table

QUIZ QUESTION:

WHAT MOVES THE WATER?

A) WATER MOLECULES ARE DRAWN TOGETHER. GRAVITY PULLS THE WATER DOWNWARDS

B) AIR PRESSURE AND GRAVITY

C) ALL OF THESE

WHAT HAPPENS?

ANSWER: C

When you suck the straw, you lower its air pressure, so water moves into it. This gets the water flowing, and the other forces keep it moving. It's known as the *siphon effect*.

DID YOU KNOW?

Toilets flush using the siphon effect. Once the water starts flowing, it doesn't stop until the tank is empty.

WATER TIGHTROPE

For this next experiment, you'll actually make water flow along a piece of string . . . .

WHAT YOU NEED

Nail

Tape measure

Scissors

String

Bucket with a handle

Plastic cup

WHAT YOU DO

1 Ask an adult to help you press the nail into the base of the plastic cup. Make a hole a little larger than the string.

2 Cut 1.5 metres of string. Wet the string and thread one end through the hole in the cup. Make a knot about 3 cm below the end. Check that the knot can't go through the hole.

3 Place the bucket in a bathtub or outside to avoid spills. Tie the other end of the string to the bucket handle.

4 Fill the cup with water. Stand far enough away from the bucket so that the string creates a straight line. Hold the cup a little higher than the bucket and make sure the string is taut.

STRING

WHAT HAPPENS?

ANSWER: C

The string is wet and water molecules cling together. Gravity pulls the water from the cup down the string.

QUIZ QUESTION:

WHAT WILL HAPPEN TO THE WATER ON THE STRING?

A) IT FLOWS UPWARDS

B) NOTHING

C) IT FLOWS DOWNWARDS

WHAT'S NEXT?

How little gravity do you need? Try the experiment with less of a slope on the string.

MAKE IT RAIN

With the help of science, you can make it rain!

WHAT YOU DO

1 Wear gloves and cover the base of the metal bowl with ice. Leave the bowl in the freezer for a few hours.

2 Ask an adult helper to boil a kettle and then allow it to cool down for 2–3 minutes.

3 Fill the clear bowl halfway with hot water and stir in one teaspoonful of salt. Dip the teaspoon in the water and taste it. The water should taste salty.

4 Wear gloves and hold the metal bowl over the clear bowl. 'Rain' will fall from the metal bowl into the water. Use the spoon to collect and taste the water.

METAL BOWL

CONDENSATION

WARNING!
BOILING WATER CAN BE DANGEROUS. ICE CAN BURN SKIN – ALWAYS WEAR GLOVES WHEN TOUCHING ICE OR COLD METAL.

SALTY WATER

CLEAR BOWL

QUIZ QUESTION:

DOES THE 'RAIN' TASTE SALTY?

A) YES—IT CAME FROM SALTY WATER

B) NO—IT'S MADE OF WATER ONLY

C) YES—BUT LESS SALTY THAN WATER IN THE GLASS BOWL

WHAT HAPPENS?

ANSWER: B

Warm water molecules have enough energy to break free from the others and float into the air. They form a type of gas called *water vapour*. This process is called *evaporation*.

Water in the bowl evaporates. When the water vapour touches the cold metal, it condenses into water (this process is called *condensation*). Salt does not evaporate, so the water doesn't taste salty.

WHAT YOU NEED

Ice cubes

Gloves

A large, clear bowl

Teaspoon

Salt

Metal bowl or plate large enough to cover the bowl

Soup spoon

DID YOU KNOW?

Evaporation and condensation create weather. Clouds are formed from water vapour from lakes and seas. As the clouds cool, the water vapour condenses into droplets. That's where rain comes from!

WATER QUIZ

ADD THE MISSING WORDS:

1) THE S_ _ _ _ _ EFFECT MAKES WATER FLOW ALONG A TUBE.

2) C_ _ _ _ _ _ _ _ FIBRES ARE FOUND IN PAPER AND PLANT STEMS.

3) AN EGG CAN FLOAT IN S_ _ _ _ WATER.

Answers: 1) Siphon, 2) Cellulose, 3) Salty

Most substances on Earth are mixtures of different molecules. In this chapter, we'll be mixing all sorts of molecules and materials... with amazing results.

MAKE BUTTER

How delicious is melted butter on hot toast? Yum!
But what's the yellow stuff made of, and how is it made?

WHAT YOU DO

1 Allow the double cream to stand at room temperature for 1 hour.

2 Ask an adult to use a blender to blend the cream. The double cream will thicken and turn crumbly. White liquid will soon appear. Stop blending when there's no more white liquid being produced.

3 Collect the yellow solids in a sieve. Over a bowl, press the yellow solids between the two large spoons to squeeze out any more liquid.

4 The yellow stuff is butter. Fill another bowl with water, then add the ice and butter. Gently press out more liquid from the butter between the spoons into the surrounding water. The butter turns crumbly. Sieve the butter from the bowl and press it into the third bowl. Squeeze out the liquid one last time. Store your butter in the fridge.

SQUEEZE OUT AS MUCH LIQUID AS POSSIBLE

BALLS OF FAT CLUMP TOGETHER

QUIZ QUESTION:

WHY WILL BLENDING THE MIXTURE MAKE BUTTER?

A) IT ALLOWS TINY BLOBS OF FAT TO CONNECT

B) IT TRIGGERS A CHEMICAL REACTION THAT BREAKS UP CREAM

C) IT MAKES CERTAIN CREAM CHEMICALS CHANGE COLOUR

WHAT HAPPENS?

ANSWER: A

Cream is water with microscopic balls of fat. The fat balls have walls that stop them merging. Shaking breaks the walls. The fat balls clump together to make butter.

WHAT YOU NEED

2 large spoons

300 ml of double cream

Blender

3 large bowls

Ice cubes

Sieve

WHAT'S NEXT?

Butter has the same density as ice. How can you prove this at Step 4?

DID YOU KNOW?

In Africa and the Middle East, it is traditional to make butter by rocking milk in a goatskin bag.

MIXTURE EXPERIMENTS

CRAZY COLOURS

Science can be colourful and even artistic. This simple experiment shows you how to turn milk into something pretty.

WHAT YOU DO

1. Cover the bowl base with milk.
2. Place droplets of food colouring in the milk. Space the drops out.
3. Dip the cotton bud into washing-up liquid.
4. Touch the milk with the cotton bud.

QUIZ QUESTION:

WHAT WILL THE COLOURS DO?

A) BUBBLE AND FLOAT UP TO THE CEILING

B) MAKE SWIRLING PATTERNS

C) FORM STRIPES

WHAT HAPPENS?

ANSWER: B

The detergent in the washing-up liquid breaks down surface tension, allowing the water and fat droplets in the milk to mix. As they mix, you see swirls in the food colouring.

The detergent molecules help water molecules and fat molecules join together. The fat molecules are very large and have to twist and move around to join with the detergent molecules. This swirls the food colouring around.

WHAT YOU NEED

Full-fat milk

Milk

Washing-up liquid

Bowl

Cotton bud

Liquid food colouring (not gel)

Use as many colours as you like!

FOOD COLOURING

SURFACE TENSION

FAT

DID YOU KNOW?

In ancient Roman times, detergents were soaps made by mixing fat and ash!

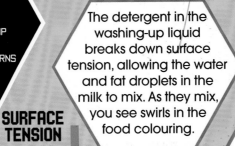

OILY LAVA LAMP

This experiment isn't really a lamp, but thanks to some clever chemistry, it looks just like one.

WHAT YOU NEED

Vegetable oil

Glass of warm water

Liquid food colouring

Salt

Torch

Teaspoon

WHAT YOU DO

1 Add liquid food colouring to the water and stir in well.

2 Pour the vegetable oil onto the surface of the water in a layer that's more than 1 cm thick.

3 Now sprinkle a spoonful of salt onto the oil. Watch what happens and then add more salt.

QUIZ QUESTION:

WHAT WILL HAPPEN TO THE OIL?

A) GLOWS IN THE DARK

B) STARTS TO SMELL BAD

C) SINKS AND THEN RISES

WHAT HAPPENS?

ANSWER: C

Oil floats because it's less dense than water. The salt grains drag oil to the bottom of the glass. Oil bubbles rise as the salt dissolves in water.

WHAT'S NEXT?

Darken the room and shine a torch through the glass. It looks just like a lava lamp!

DID YOU KNOW?

Oil and water don't mix because water molecules are more attracted to each other than to the oil molecules.

MIXTURE EXPERIMENTS

POP BAG

This is a messy experiment that's guaranteed to go off with a bang!

WHAT YOU DO

1 Heap 1.5 tablespoons of bicarbonate of soda on a sheet of kitchen paper. Fold the paper around the powder to form a small packet.

2 Mix 150 ml of vinegar in the measuring jug with 75 ml of warm water. Take the plastic bag outside and pour the mixture into it.

3 Drop the bicarbonate of soda packet into the plastic bag and quickly seal it up.

4 Shake the bag as fast as you can, then drop the bag, stand back, and enjoy the show!

WHAT YOU NEED

Bicarbonate of soda

Tablespoon

Kitchen paper

Vinegar

Small resealable plastic bag

Measuring jug

DROP PACKET INTO BAG

QUIZ QUESTION:

WHAT DO YOU THINK WILL HAPPEN TO THE BAG?

A) THE BAG FILLS WITH GAS AND WATER UNTIL IT BURSTS

B) THE BAG HEATS UP – THIS INCREASES AIR PRESSURE

C) KITCHEN PAPER EXPLODES WHEN MIXED WITH BICARBONATE OF SODA

WHAT HAPPENS?

ANSWER: A

This experiment is a *chemical reaction*. That's when **atoms** or molecules combine to form new molecules.

The bicarbonate of soda reacts with the acid in the vinegar, creating more water and carbon dioxide gas. The carbon dioxide gas fills the bag until it pops.

WHAT'S NEXT?

Try the experiment with more or less bicarbonate of soda. Will it work if you leave out the water?

DID YOU KNOW?

Bicarbonate of soda is an ingredient of natron. This was the substance used to dry out Egyptian mummies!

MAKE PEANUT BUTTER

Here's a fantastic edible experiment that's tasty AND scientific!

MIXTURE EXPERIMENTS

WHAT YOU NEED

- 1.5 tablespoons of sunflower oil
- 1.5 tablespoons of honey
- Blender
- Teaspoon
- 200g of dry roasted peanuts
- Stopwatch

WHAT YOU DO

1 Ask an adult to help you blend the dry roasted peanuts and honey for 60 seconds. Taste a little and note the texture.

2 Add oil and blend until smooth and creamy.

3 Taste a little and note the texture. Add a little oil if the mixture seems too dry.

4 Cool the mixture in a fridge for two hours.

QUIZ QUESTION:

WHAT WILL HAPPEN TO THE MIXTURE AT STEP 4?

A) IT BECOMES SOFT AND RUNNY
B) IT GETS THICK AND HARD
C) IT SLOWLY TURNS GREEN

WHAT HAPPENS?

ANSWER: B

This experiment is about mixing and changing materials. Blending breaks up the plant **cells**, releasing peanut oil that mixes with sunflower oil and honey. Cooling oil molecules form clumps that thicken the mixture.

DID YOU KNOW?

Peanuts aren't technically nuts because they don't grow on trees. They're more closely related to beans or peas and grow underground.

EDIBLE GAS

Did you know that it's possible to make your own edible gas? Try this experiment to give your mouth a tasty treat!

WHAT YOU DO

1. Line the baking tray with tin foil and grease with margarine. Place the baking tray in the fridge for 30 minutes.

2. An adult should heat the sugar and two teaspoons of water in the saucepan. The sugar turns runny, then dry and then brown. When the mixture turns brown, add another two teaspoons of water.

3. When the sugar starts to bubble, an adult should add a teaspoon of baking powder. They need to stir the mixture well.

4. Now pour the mixture into the baking tray.

5. Allow the mixture to cool. Hold it to the light and examine with a magnifying glass.

WHAT YOU NEED

Magnifying glass

100g of caster sugar

4 teaspoons of water

Measuring jug

Saucepan

Baking powder

Teaspoon

Tin foil

Margarine

Baking Tray

QUIZ QUESTION:

WHERE DO THE BUBBLES COME FROM?

A) BOILING SUGAR AND WATER

B) A CHEMICAL REACTION CAUSED BY BAKING POWDER

C) SOMEONE MUST HAVE DRIBBLED IN MY EXPERIMENT

WHAT HAPPENS?

ANSWER: B

Baking powder reacts with water to make carbon dioxide gas. The gooey cooling sugar traps air bubbles made by the gas.

WARNING!

BEWARE OF HEAT. ADULT HELP IS VITAL! A GROWN-UP CAN CLEAN THE SAUCEPAN BY BOILING WATER IN IT.

THE ACID TEST

Vinegar is slightly acidic and tastes tingly on your tongue. But is it possible to test acid without actually tasting it?

WHAT YOU NEED

Baking powder

100% red grape juice

3 glasses

Measuring jug

Teaspoon

Lemon juice

WHAT YOU DO

1 Pour 100 ml of grape juice into the first glass and then rinse out the measuring jug.

2 Pour 50 ml of lemon juice into the second glass. Stir in 50-ml of grape juice. Rinse out the measuring jug again.

3 Add 50 ml of water to the third glass and stir in one heaping teaspoon of baking powder. Stir regularly until the mixture no longer fizzes when stirred.

4 Add 50-ml of grape juice to the third glass and stir again.

5 Compare the colour of each liquid.

WHAT HAPPENS?

ANSWER: C

The lemon juice turns the grape juice pinkish (2) and the baking powder turns the grape juice purplish (3). The grape juice glass reminds you of the original colour (1). This is called a *control*.

Acids and alkalis alter colour molecules in the juice. Baking powder is a type of base called an alkali, and lemon juice contains an acid.

QUIZ QUESTION:

WHAT WILL HAPPEN TO THE COLOURS?

A) THE COLOURS IN THE LIQUIDS MIX TO MAKE NEW COLOURS

B) STIRRING THE JUICE CHANGES ITS COLOUR

C) THERE'S A CHEMICAL REACTION AFFECTING THE COLOUR

DID YOU KNOW?

A substance that changes colour with acid or alkali is called an **indicator**. Other vegetable dyes such as beetroot juice and red cabbage juice also work as indicators.

1 CONTROL (GRAPE JUICE)

2 WITH LEMON JUICE

3 WITH BAKING POWDER

GAS BALLOON

Our atmosphere consists of all sorts of different gases. Here's an easy scientific way to make your own.

MIXTURE EXPERIMENTS

White vinegar

Baking powder

250-ml glass bottle

2 balloons

Funnel

Teaspoon

WHAT YOU DO

1 Use the funnel to add two teaspoonfuls of baking powder to the bottle. Rinse the funnel with water.

2 Use the funnel to fill the second balloon up to its neck with vinegar.

3 Stretch the balloon over the bottle's neck, but don't allow any vinegar into the bottle just yet.

4 Place the bottle in a sink and lift the balloon so that the vinegar pours into the bottle.

5 Watch the balloon inflate and then tie the end. Blow up the second balloon so it is the same size as the first balloon. Compare the weight of both balloons in your hands.

BALLOON INFLATES

QUIZ QUESTION:

WHICH BALLOON IS HEAVIER?

A) THE CONTROL BALLOON

B) THE BALLOON FROM THE BOTTLE

C) THEY BOTH WEIGH THE SAME

WHAT HAPPENS?

ANSWER: B

The balloon fills with carbon dioxide gas from a reaction between baking powder and vinegar.

The heavier-than-air gas makes the balloon a little heavier than an identical balloon containing the same amount of air.

DID YOU KNOW?

Plants use carbon dioxide gas, water and sunlight to make food in their leaves. This is called **photosynthesis**.

MAKE ORANGE SODA

This refreshingly simple experiment shows you how to add plenty of fizz to your very own tasty fruit drinks!

WHAT YOU NEED

- **Bicarbonate of soda**
- **Teaspoon**
- **Glass**
- **100% orange juice**
- **Water**

WHAT YOU DO

1. Pour half a glass of orange juice.
2. Top the glass off with water.
3. Stir in one teaspoonful of bicarbonate of soda.

QUIZ QUESTION:

WHY DID YOU ADD WATER AT STEP 2?

A) WATER AND BICARBONATE OF SODA ARE NEEDED FOR THE REACTION WITH THE ACID IN THE ORANGE JUICE

B) THE WATER STOPS THE CHEMICAL REACTION FROM GOING OUT OF CONTROL AND BLOWING UP YOUR HOUSE

C) TO STOP THE DRINK FROM BEING TOO SWEET

WHAT HAPPENS?

ANSWER: A

Orange juice contains the same acid as lemon juice. If you've tried the Pop Bag experiment on page 36, you may remember the chemical reaction.

Bicarbonate of soda reacts with the water and the acid in the orange juice, releasing carbon dioxide gas. In this experiment, the gas stays in the drink and makes it fizzy.

DID YOU KNOW?

Too much fizz? In the late 1800s, people were still experimenting with fizzy drinks – the gas pressure sometimes made the bottles explode!

MAKE PLASTIC

So far we've had science experiments you can eat and drink. Now here's how to make plastic in your very own kitchen!

WHAT YOU DO

1. Ask an adult to heat the milk in a saucepan until it starts to simmer.

2. The adult should then pour the milk into the bowl.

3. Stir in 4 teaspoonfuls of vinegar. White lumps will form.

4. Sift out the white lumps. Rinse the lumps in water and press them together in a clean cloth or paper towel. Hey presto, you've made plastic!

QUIZ QUESTION:

WHAT WOULD HAPPEN IF YOU USED A DIFFERENT ACID SUCH AS LEMON JUICE?

A) THE MILK WOULD STILL FORM LUMPS

B) NO LUMPS FORM

C) THE LEMON JUICE WOULD MAKE THE MILK TURN YELLOW

WHAT HAPPENS?

ANSWER: A

Milk contains casein molecules. Casein is found in cheese. The molecule is normally rolled into tight balls, but the acid makes it unravel like string.

The stringy molecules form lumps. All plastics are made of long molecules called **polymers** that are easy to mold.

PRESS LUMPS TOGETHER

WHAT'S NEXT?

Try adding food colouring to the milk after warming, but before adding the vinegar.

DID YOU KNOW?

Before 1945, milk casein was often used to make plastic. The plastic was made into buttons or jewellery!

WHAT YOU NEED

Bowl

Vinegar

Wooden spoon

125 ml of milk

Measuring jug

Milk

Teaspoon

Clean cloth or kitchen paper

Saucepan

Sieve

MIXTURES QUIZ

1) WHICH SUBSTANCE CONTAINS A BASE?

2) WHICH SUBSTANCE CONTAINS AN ACID?

3) WHICH THREE SUBSTANCES CAN YOU MIX TO MAKE CARBON DIOXIDE?

A Water

B Sugar

C Vinegar

D Salt

E Bicarbonate of soda

F Cheese

Answers: 1) E, 2) C, 3) A, C, E.

ENERGY & SOUND EXPERIMENTS

31

Energy is all around us – it's the power we need to get things moving. Energy can take many forms, including heat, sound and even your favourite music.

PEN TOP LAUNCHER

Energy can change form and be stored. That's the secret behind this experiment.

WHAT YOU DO

1 Ask an adult to help you make a hole on one side of the tube about one third of the way down and another hole on the opposite side of the tube.

2 Stick two pieces of sticky tape over the outside of each hole in the tube. Then make a hole in the tape.

3 Thread the rubber band through the holes in the tube. You'll need a small screwdriver or something similar to push the band through the holes. Put a pencil through each side of the band and secure with more sticky tape, as shown.

4 Place the pen top on the rubber band, pull back, and release. Watch that pen top go!

WHAT YOU NEED

- Plastic pen top
- Strong cardboard tube
- Scissors
- Small screwdriver
- Large rubber band
- Large sticky tape or packing tape
- 2 pencils

WARNING!
DON'T AIM AT PEOPLE OR ANIMALS!

CARDBOARD TUBE

PEN TOP

RUBBER BAND

PENCIL

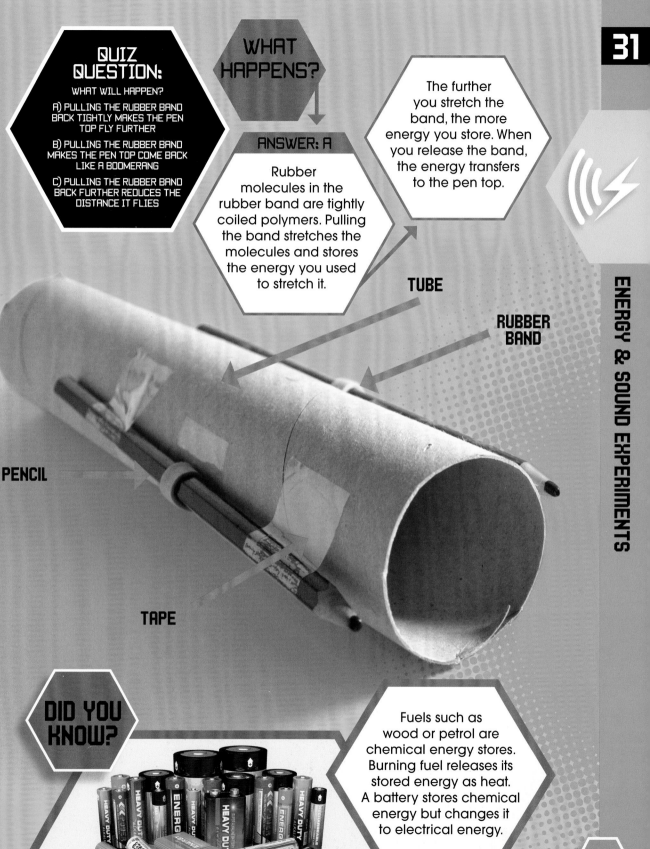

ENERGY & SOUND EXPERIMENTS

QUIZ QUESTION:

WHAT WILL HAPPEN?

A) PULLING THE RUBBER BAND BACK TIGHTLY MAKES THE PEN TOP FLY FURTHER

B) PULLING THE RUBBER BAND MAKES THE PEN TOP COME BACK LIKE A BOOMERANG

C) PULLING THE RUBBER BAND BACK FURTHER REDUCES THE DISTANCE IT FLIES

WHAT HAPPENS?

ANSWER: A

Rubber molecules in the rubber band are tightly coiled polymers. Pulling the band stretches the molecules and stores the energy you used to stretch it.

The further you stretch the band, the more energy you store. When you release the band, the energy transfers to the pen top.

TUBE

RUBBER BAND

PENCIL

TAPE

DID YOU KNOW?

Fuels such as wood or petrol are chemical energy stores. Burning fuel releases its stored energy as heat. A battery stores chemical energy but changes it to electrical energy.

MAKING SOLUTIONS

Heat energy doesn't just get water moving.
It affects chemical reactions, too....

WHAT YOU DO

1 Fill the jug with water and add some ice cubes.

2 Leave the water jug to chill in the fridge for two hours. Add 250 ml of hot water to one glass and 250 ml of cold water from the fridge to the other glass.

3 Using separate spoons, add one teaspoonful of salt to each glass. Stir well to dissolve as much salt as you can.

QUIZ QUESTION:

WHERE WILL THE SALT DISSOLVE BEST?

A) HOT WATER

B) COLD WATER

C) NEITHER – BUT THE COLD GLASS STARTS TO STEAM

WHAT YOU NEED

Jug

Measuring jug

2 clear glasses

2 tea or soup spoons

Salt

Ice cubes

Sugar

COLD WATER

ANSWER: A

Water molecules pull the salt crystal particles apart for the salt to dissolve. At a higher temperature, the water molecules move faster and hit the crystals more often. This dissolves the salt crystals more quickly.

WHAT HAPPENS?

WHAT'S NEXT?

Try using sugar instead of salt. Does sugar dissolve more easily? If so, why?

HOT WATER

SALT

AIR ENERGY

How does heat energy affect air trapped in a balloon? Here's one way to find out!

WHAT YOU NEED

2 balloons

Cardboard box

WHAT YOU DO

1 Blow up both balloons to half their maximum size. The balloons must be the same size.

2 Put one balloon in the freezer for 20 minutes.

3 Put the other balloon in the box and leave it in a warm place, like on top of a radiator.

QUIZ QUESTION:

WHAT WILL HAPPEN TO THE BALLOONS?

A) THE COLD BALLOON SHRINKS AND THE WARM BALLOON GETS BIGGER

B) THE COLD BALLOON GETS BIGGER AND THE WARM BALLOON SHRINKS

C) THE WARM BALLOON TURNS PINK AND THE COLD BALLOON TURNS BLUE

WHAT HAPPENS?

ANSWER: A

As air warms up, molecules move faster and move apart, so the balloon expands. As air cools down, molecules move more slowly and become closer together, so the balloon shrinks.

Warm air is less dense than cold air, and this makes warm air rise. This is how a hot air balloon is able to lift off!

DID YOU KNOW?

ENERGY & SOUND EXPERIMENTS

MAKE YOUR OWN HEAT

Feeling chilly? Here's a simple scientific experiment to warm you up!

WHAT YOU NEED

2 sticks

WHAT YOU DO

1. Touch the two sticks to your face. Feel how warm they are.
2. Rub them together for 30 seconds and repeat Step 1.

RUB STICKS TOGETHER

QUIZ QUESTION:

WHAT WILL HAPPEN TO THE STICKS?

A) BOTH STICKS ARE COOLER

B) BOTH STICKS GLOW RED HOT

C) BOTH STICKS FEEL WARMER

WHAT HAPPENS?

ANSWER: C

Energy changes form all the time. When molecules rub together, some of their movement energy turns into heat energy.

This rubbing force is called **friction**. It's friction that warms the sticks.

DID YOU KNOW?

One traditional way to make fire involves rubbing sticks together. Don't try to make fire without an adult helper!

WHAT'S NEXT?

Friction is everywhere. See how much heat you can make by rubbing different surfaces. Why do rough surfaces produce more heat?

FLOATING WATER

This great experiment adds heat energy to water with colourful results.

WHAT YOU NEED

- 50-ml bottle
- Deep clear jug of water
- Liquid food colouring (not gel)

WHAT YOU DO

1 Leave the jug of water in the fridge for a few hours.

2 Add a few drops of colouring to the small bottle and then top it off with hot tap water.

3 Place the small bottle at the bottom of the larger jug.

WARNING!
ASK AN ADULT FOR HELP WHEN USING HOT WATER IN EXPERIMENTS.

WHAT HAPPENS?

QUIZ QUESTION:
WHAT WILL HAPPEN?
A) THE HOT WATER RISES UP
B) NOTHING – HOT AND COLD WATER DON'T MIX
C) THE BOTTLE WILL EXPLODE

ANSWER: A

Heat energy makes the molecules in the water move faster and further apart. This makes the water expand and become less dense than cold water. The hot water rises and the colder, denser water sinks to fill the gap.

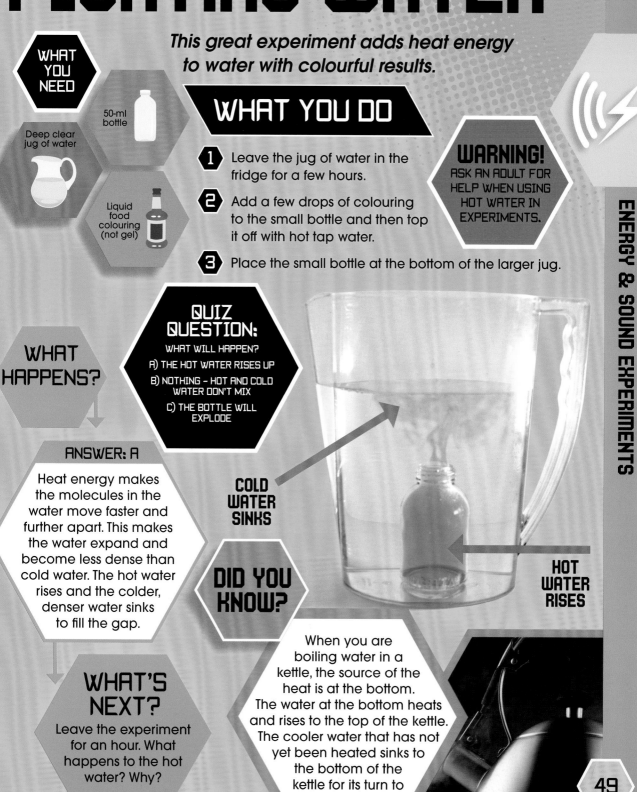

COLD WATER SINKS

HOT WATER RISES

DID YOU KNOW?

When you are boiling water in a kettle, the source of the heat is at the bottom. The water at the bottom heats and rises to the top of the kettle. The cooler water that has not yet been heated sinks to the bottom of the kettle for its turn to be warmed.

WHAT'S NEXT?
Leave the experiment for an hour. What happens to the hot water? Why?

WARM AND COZY

When you shiver, you lose heat energy. Here's how to stay cozy by hanging on to heat energy!

ENERGY & SOUND EXPERIMENTS

WHAT YOU DO

1. Fill both jars to the brim with hot tap water. Place the lids on the jars.

2. Wrap one jar tightly in foil and place the glove on top of it. Wrap the glove tightly in more foil.

3. Place both jars in the freezer for one hour.

WHAT YOU NEED

2 glass jars (about 43 ml) with screw-on lids

Tin foil

Thick glove

QUIZ QUESTION:

WHAT WILL HAPPEN TO THE WRAPPED-UP WATER?
A) IT'S FROZEN SOLID
B) IT'S LUKEWARM
C) IT STAYS HOT

WHAT HAPPENS?

ANSWER: B

Heat energy always moves to colder regions. The wrapped-up water retains heat energy because foil **reflects** it back into the jar. The glove traps air, which is a good heat insulator. This traps heat in the jar and keeps it warm for longer.

WARNING!

ASK AN ADULT FOR HELP WHEN USING HOT WATER IN EXPERIMENTS.

Birds fluff up their feathers on a cold winter's day to trap extra air. The fluffed-up feathers are a better heat insulator and help keep the birds warmer.

GLOVE WRAPPED IN FOIL

DID YOU KNOW?

SCIENCE SCREAM

This experiment will turn sound energy into a spooky scream!

WHAT YOU DO

1 Ask an adult to help you make a hole in the cup base just large enough for the string.

2 Use the pencil point to push the string through the hole as shown below. Knot the string twice to secure it in the cup.

3 Wet the string, then tie the other end to a door handle.

4 Stretch the string taut. Rub your thumb and forefinger quickly along the string.

WHAT YOU NEED

Sharp pencil

Large plastic cup

1 metre of string

Scissors

QUIZ QUESTION:

WHAT WILL MAKE THE SCREAM?

A) YOU – WHEN YOU GET AN ELECTRIC SHOCK!

B) SOUND ENERGY STORED IN THE STRING

C) VIBRATIONS ON THE STRING

WHAT HAPPENS?

ANSWER: C

The movement energy of your fingers makes the string vibrate. The vibrations pass to the cup and the air it holds. Waves of vibration pass through the air, and you hear them as sound.

WHAT'S NEXT?

Does the sound rise or fall with the speed of your fingers? Why?

SINGING GLASSES

Is it really possible to make a glass sing?

WHAT YOU NEED

2 large glasses

WHAT YOU DO

1. Make sure your hands are very clean.
2. Pour water into one glass until it is halfway full.
3. Wet your finger and run it firmly and quickly around the rim of the empty glass.
4. Repeat Step 3 for the half-full glass.

QUIZ QUESTION:

WHAT WILL HAPPEN?

A) THE EMPTY GLASS SINGS. THE GLASS WITH WATER IS SILENT

B) BOTH GLASSES SING – THE GLASS WITH WATER MAKES A LOWER SOUND

C) THE EMPTY GLASS MAKES A RUDE NOISE THAT SOUNDS VERY FUNNY!

WHAT HAPPENS?

ANSWER: B

The experiment turns movement energy into sound energy. As your finger slides and stops along the rim, it sets off vibrations in the glass.

These vibrations make sound waves. If you don't hear anything, keep trying. The glass with water is heavier and vibrates more slowly. Slower vibrations cause sound waves to be more widely spaced, and you hear them as deeper sounds.

DID YOU KNOW?

An instrument called a glass harmonica makes sounds in this way. At one time, its music was thought (incorrectly) to drive people mad!

SEEING SOUND

You can't actually see sound waves – at least, not until you make them visible....

WHAT YOU DO

1 Cover the top of the bin with clingfilm and use the rubber band or sticky tape to keep it stretched as tightly as possible.

2 Scatter a half teaspoon of salt on the clingfilm.

3 Turn the small can upside down 10-15 cm above the clingfilm. Hit its base with the wooden spoon.

Clingfilm

Empty metal can

Large rubber band or sticky tape

Metal bin or large container

Teaspoon

Wooden spoon

Salt

ENERGY & SOUND EXPERIMENTS

QUIZ QUESTION:

WHAT WILL HAPPEN TO THE SALT?

A) THE SALT MOVES AROUND

B) THE SALT GIVES OFF AN UNPLEASANT SMELL

C) THE BIN DANCES ABOUT ON ITS OWN

10-15 CM

WHAT HAPPENS?

DID YOU KNOW?

ANSWER: A

Sound waves from the can hit the clingfilm and make it vibrate. The vibrations are hard to see, but you can observe the salt moving as a result.

In 2014, Japanese scientists used sound waves to make small objects float in the air. The scientists used four sets of speakers pointing towards a single point. The speakers moved the objects in mid-air!

REFLECT SOUND

Here's how to bounce sound around and turn an ordinary umbrella into an ear!

WHAT YOU DO

1 Set up the frying pan and timer on the chair using sticky tape and string as shown on page 55.

2 Start the timer and move to the other side of the room with the umbrella.

3 Point the umbrella handle towards the timer and listen with your head inside the umbrella. Try and get your ear close to the handle.

QUIZ QUESTION:

WHAT WILL YOU HEAR?

A) I HEARD TICKING AT STEP 2, BUT NOT STEP 3

B) I HEARD TICKING AT STEP 2 AND IT WAS FASTER AT STEP 3

C) I HEARD TICKING AT STEP 3, BUT NOT SO WELL AT STEP 2

WHAT HAPPENS?

ANSWER: C

Sound waves can be reflected and redirected. The pan collects sound waves and directs them towards the umbrella.

The umbrella collects the sound waves and sends them towards your unblocked ear.

WHAT'S NEXT?

Can you hear the ticking 15 metres away? Is it still as loud?

WHAT YOU NEED

Large frying pan or wok

String

Scissors

Tape measure

Chair

Wide sticky tape

Umbrella

Kitchen timer

DID YOU KNOW?

Your ears collect sound waves in much the same way as the umbrella. They redirect sound waves towards your ear holes. Sound waves reach each ear from slightly different directions. Your brain compares data and uses it to judge the direction of the sound.

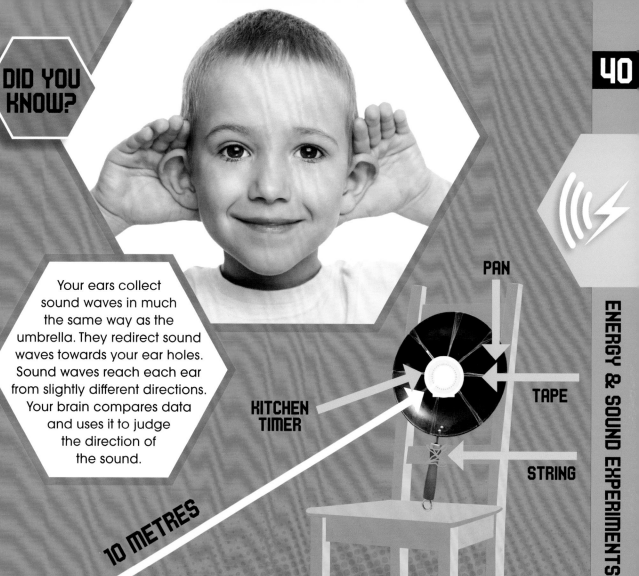

PAN

TAPE

STRING

KITCHEN TIMER

10 METRES

ENERGY & SOUND QUIZ

CAN YOU MATCH THE ENERGY TO THE ITEM?

1) CHANGES CHEMICAL ENERGY INTO ELECTRICAL ENERGY
2) TURNS MOVEMENT ENERGY INTO SOUND WAVES
3) HAS A LOT OF HEAT ENERGY

 A

 B

 C

Answers:1) C, 2) B, 3) A.

Forces are all about movement – they explain how and why things move. They also make great science experiments!

ROCKET BALLOON

You'll be amazed to discover that a balloon filled with air can blast along just like a rocket!

WHAT YOU DO

1. Set up the two chairs 5 metres apart.

2. Cut 6 metres of string. Tie one end of the string to the top of one of the chairs.

3. Thread the straw through the string and tie the other end of the string to the top of the second chair.

4. Blow up the balloon and let it go three times. Blow it up a fourth time and secure it to the straw with sticky tape while holding the balloon neck closed.

5. Set up the experiment so the balloon neck is close to one chair and then let the balloon go.

QUIZ QUESTION:

WHAT WILL HAPPEN TO THE BALLOON?

A) THE BALLOON WHIZZES TO THE FAR END OF THE STRING

B) THE BALLOON REACHES THE FAR END AND MOVES BACK ALONG THE STRING

C) THE BALLOON POPS

5 METRES

STRING

TAPE

TAPE

STRAW

WHAT HAPPENS?

ANSWER: A

When you compress air in the balloon, the air pushes back. Sir Isaac Newton's third law of motion shows that any force creates an equal force in the opposite direction.

This is why air blasting backwards from the balloon pushes the balloon forward.

WHAT'S NEXT?

Repeat the experiment twice, each time with less air in the balloon. How does this affect the balloon's speed and travel distance?

WHAT YOU NEED

Balloon

2 chairs

Sticky Tape

Measuring tape

Scissors

Drinking straw

String

DID YOU KNOW?

Rockets and jet engines work like your experiment. The force comes from burning fuel and hot gases, which are blasted backwards. This propels the rocket or jet forward.

MOVE A BOTTLE

This is a great party trick to impress your friends. Just don't forget to keep the bottle top on!

WHAT YOU DO

1. Use the pencil to make a small hole in the card 2.5 cm from the bottom.

2. Cut 84 cm of string and tie a knot through the hole.

3. Place the card on a smooth table and the bottle on top of the card. Don't open the bottle.

4. Gently pull the string, then give the string a quick tug.

INERTIA

FRICTION BETWEEN THE BOTTLE AND PAPER

WHAT YOU NEED

Pencil

500 ml plastic bottle of water

Scissors

A4 card

String

Ruler

Table

Sandpaper

QUIZ QUESTION:

WHAT WILL HAPPEN WHEN YOU TUG THE STRING?

A) THE BOTTLE FLIES THROUGH THE AIR

B) THE BOTTLE FALLS ON THE FLOOR – LUCKY I LEFT THE TOP ON!

C) THE BOTTLE DOESN'T MOVE

WHAT HAPPENS?

ANSWER: C

Inertia tries to keep the bottle where it is. But friction between the bottle and the card tries to keep the bottle on the card.

When you pull the string gently, friction wins and the bottle moves with the card. But the friction is weak. A rapid tug on the string overcomes friction and inertia keeps the bottle where it is.

WHAT'S NEXT?

Try sticking sandpaper over the card. Why won't the experiment work?

ON A ROLL

When balls bump and bash into each other, it's the science of momentum that's all-important....

WHAT YOU NEED

- 22 x 28 cm card
- Tape measure
- Books to stack 13 cm high
- Scissors
- Modelling clay
- Marbles (or other balls of different sizes)

WHAT YOU DO

1 Fold the card in half lengthways and cut along the fold. You should be left with two pieces, each about 11 cm wide.

2 Fold each side of each piece of card in 2.5 cm to make U-shaped channels.

3 Set up the experiment as shown, with a blob of modelling clay under the channel to hold it in place.

4 Place the small marble at the base of the slope and roll the large marble from the top. Swap the marbles around and repeat.

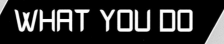

FOLD
2.5 CM
5 CM
2.5 CM

QUIZ QUESTION:

WHAT WILL HAPPEN?

A) THE LITTLE MARBLE KNOCKS THE BIG MARBLE FURTHER

B) THE BIG MARBLE KNOCKS THE LITTLE MARBLE FURTHER

C) THE LITTLE MARBLE HITS THE BIG MARBLE AND REBOUNDS UP THE RAMP

ANSWER: B

A moving marble has momentum, which depends on its speed multiplied by its mass.

WHAT HAPPENS?

The larger marble has more **mass**, so it also has greater momentum. It makes the smaller marble move further when it hits it.

WHAT'S NEXT?

Is size important? Try rolling a small, heavy ball down to hit a large, light ball.

13 CM

MARBLE

CARD CHANNEL

MODELLING CLAY

AIR BALL

By combining air pressure and force, you'll have the power to move objects.

FORCE EXPERIMENTS

WHAT YOU NEED

Empty 2-litre plastic bottle (with top removed)

Polystyrene ball

Funnel (big enough for the ball to fit inside)

Bendy straw

WHAT YOU DO

1. Balance the polystyrene ball on the bottle.

2. Clap your hands on the sides of the bottle. The ball should fly up into the air.

3. Now place the funnel in the bottle and the ball inside the funnel.

4. Repeat Step 2.

QUIZ QUESTION:

WHAT WILL HAPPEN AT STEP 4?

A) THE BALL DOESN'T GO ANYWHERE

B) THE BALL FLIES IN A FIGURE OF EIGHT

C) THE BALL HEATS UP AND STARTS STEAMING

WHAT HAPPENS?

ANSWER: A

At Step 2 the force of air pressure raises the ball like the rocket on page 15. When the ball's in the funnel, the air speeds up to get around it.

Faster air has a lower pressure, and so the pressure below the ball is lower than pressure above it. The ball is held in the funnel by the air pressure of the room.

AIR PRESSURE

WHAT'S NEXT?

Try this experiment using a bendy straw instead of a bottle. Bend the straw and blow through the longer end. Can you make the polystyrene ball hover? Why does the ball spin?

AIR FLOW

AIR FLOW

COIN ON A TRAY

Find out about inertia by taking a coin for a ride!

WHAT YOU NEED

Modelling clay

Pencil

A4 card

Light coin

WHAT YOU DO

1. Place the card on a smooth surface or floor.
2. Roll a 2.5 cm blob of modelling clay and stick it to the card.
3. Place the coin in the middle of the card.
4. Use the modelling clay as a handle to push the card forwards, before suddenly swerving left or right.

COIN

MODELLING CLAY

QUIZ QUESTION:

WHAT WILL HAPPEN TO THE COIN?

A) IT BARELY MOVES

B) IT FLIES OFF THE CARD IN THE SAME DIRECTION AS YOUR TURN

C) IT FLIES OFF IN THE OPPOSITE DIRECTION OF YOUR TURN

WHAT HAPPENS?

ANSWER: C

Sir Isaac Newton's first law of motion shows that things don't move until a force acts on them. Then they move in a straight line until forced to change direction.

This quality is inertia. Inertia makes the coin move in a straight line, instead of swerving with the card.

WHAT'S NEXT?

Repeat the experiment with heavier coins. Do they move as far?

DID YOU KNOW?

When a car brakes sharply, the people inside are thrown forwards due to their inertia. Seatbelts save people from harm.

BALLOON HOVERCRAFT

Here's how to float objects on a cushion of air!

FORCE EXPERIMENTS

WHAT YOU DO

1 Stretch the balloon neck over one end of the spool.

2 Stick the other end of the spool to the CD with a ring of modelling clay.

3 Blow up the balloon from the CD end. Hold the balloon neck so air doesn't escape.

4 Place the CD on a smooth surface and then release the balloon.

WHAT YOU NEED

Spool of thread

Unwanted CD

Balloon

Modelling clay

SPOOL

MODELLING CLAY

QUIZ QUESTION:

WHAT WILL HAPPEN TO THE CD?

A) THE CD TAKES OFF LIKE A FLYING SAUCER

B) THE CD SPINS ON THE SPOT VERY FAST

C) THE CD MOVES AROUND

ANSWER: C

WHAT HAPPENS?

Air escaping from the balloon forms a layer between the CD and the surface, reducing friction. This enables the CD to hover slightly and move easily across a smooth surface.

DID YOU KNOW?

Like your hovercraft, a real hovercraft floats on a cushion of air. The hovercraft was invented in 1956 by Christopher Cockerell following tests with old cans and a hair dryer!

PAPER STRENGTH TEST

You can't support a book with just two sheets of paper… or can you?

WHAT YOU DO

WHAT YOU NEED

Sticky Tape

Books

Scissors

2 sheets of paper

4 rubber bands

Ruler

1 Fold one piece of paper lengthways. Cut along the fold.

2 Make two pillars by rolling two half-sheets sideways as shown. Secure the edges with sticky tape and add rubber bands for support.

3 Fold up the second sheet of paper 2.5 cm from one end. Turn the paper and fold it down for the next 2.5 cm Firmly fold the entire sheet up or down until the end.

4 Place the pillars 13 cm apart and place the folded paper on top. Then put a book on top of the paper.

13 CM

QUIZ QUESTION:
WHAT WILL HAPPEN?
A) THE PAPER SUPPORTS THE BOOK
B) THE BOOK SWAYS FROM SIDE TO SIDE
C) THE BOOK SQUASHES EVERYTHING

WHAT HAPPENS?

ANSWER: A

The folds in the paper make it stiff like cardboard. It will bend easily in one direction, but not the other.

Each pillar takes the force and spreads it evenly around its circumference.

WHAT'S NEXT?
How many books can the paper structure support? Can the rolls carry weight if laid on their side? If not, why not?

LEAN ON ME

Can you hold up the Leaning Tower of Pisa using the amazing power of force?

WHAT YOU NEED

- Pen
- Long cardboard tube
- Ruler
- Modelling clay
- Felt-tip pens or paint
- Scissors

WHAT YOU DO

1. Make a 1.5 cm vertical cut at one end of the tube.

2. Mark the tube base opposite the cut. Link your mark and the top of the cut with a curved dotted line on both sides.

3. Lay the tube down and cut along the dotted lines. You can decorate your tube like the Leaning Tower of Pisa if you'd like.

4. Stand your tower on its cut end and then blow. The leaning tower falls easily.

5. Stick a 4 cm ball of modelling clay inside the tower on the long side. The ball should be 0.5 cm above the tower base. Now try blowing again.

CUT

QUIZ QUESTION:

WHAT WILL HAPPEN WHEN YOU BLOW?

A) THE TOWER FALLS IN A DIFFERENT DIRECTION

B) THE TOWER DOESN'T FALL

C) THE TOWER TURNS AROUND

WHAT HAPPENS?

ANSWER: B

Gravity tries to pull the tower down in the direction that it leans at Step 4. It's easy to blow the tower down, especially in this direction.

A weight at the tower base pulls the tower downwards and counter-balances the leaning force.

WHAT'S NEXT?

Move the weight towards the top of the tower. What happens now and why?

DID YOU KNOW?

The Leaning Tower of Pisa took 199 years to build. It leans because it was built in soft soil with shallow foundations!

GLUE BOOKS WITHOUT GLUE

Paper can be a lot stronger than you think!

WHAT YOU NEED

2 paperback books

WHAT YOU DO

1. Place one book right-side up and the other upside-down on a table.
2. Open both books and fan out the pages. Interweave every 4–5 pages of the books until all of the pages have been interwoven.
3. Lift the books and then try to pull them apart.

BOOK 1   BOOK 2

QUIZ QUESTION:
WHAT FORCE WILL STICK THE BOOKS TOGETHER?
A) MAGNETISM
B) FRICTION
C) AIR PRESSURE

WHAT HAPPENS?

ANSWER: B
The spines of the books make the force by pressing down on the pages. Friction between any two pages is small, but the number of interwoven pages multiplies the force.

DID YOU KNOW?

WHAT'S NEXT?
Try interweaving fewer pages. When can you separate the books?

The largest atlas in the world was published in 2012. Earth Platinum measures 1.8 by 1.4 metres in size!

MAKE A STUNT

Here's a fantastic scientific challenge –
build and test your very own stunt jet!

WHAT YOU DO

1 Fold the card lengthways and then cut the folded card as shown below, with the folded edge at the top.

5 CM

13 CM

4 CM

10 CM

FOLD FOR WINGS   2.5 CM   1.3 CM   8 CM

2.5 CM   1.3 CM   3 CM

2 Fold the card down along the dotted lines to make the wings. Open out the card. Cut a leftover piece of card like this.

3 CM

10 CM

7.5 CM   3 CM   2 CM

25.5 CM

3 This will be the jet fuselage and tail fin. Place the fuselage between the wings and secure with staples. Add a paperclip as shown.

PAPERCLIP   STAPLES

4 Cut and fold the tail and wings to add ailerons and the rudder.

FOLD

RUDDER

AILERONS

8.6 CM

8.6 CM   8.6 CM

8.6 CM

1.3 CM   4 CM   4 CM   ½ IN.

WHAT HAPPENS?

QUIZ QUESTION:

WHAT WILL HAPPEN WHEN YOU BEND THE AILERONS UP?

A) THE PLANE FLIES UP

B) THE PLANE FLIES DOWN

C) THE PLANE LOOPS THE LOOP

ANSWER: A

Planes fly because of a force called *lift* caused by the air pressure under the plane. Raising ailerons increases lift and the plane flies up.

DID YOU KNOW?

Your stunt jet is a type known as 'delta wing' for its wing shape. Delta wings are most commonly seen on military aircraft and are ideal for supersonic flight (faster than the speed of sound).

JET PLANE

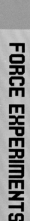

WHAT'S NEXT?

Try adjusting the positions of the ailerons and rudder. How can you make the plane fly downwards? Can you make one wing dip and the other lift or make the plane turn to one side?

Your plane is fast because its streamlined shape reduces friction with the air. This friction is called *drag*.

WHAT YOU NEED

Pencil

A4 card

Paperclip

Stapler

Ruler

Scissors

RUDDER

AILERONS

FORCE QUIZ

CAN YOU FIND THE MISSING WORDS?

1) THE QUALITY OF I _ _ _ _ _ _ MAKES IT HARD TO MOVE AN OBJECT.

2) THE FORCE OF F_ _ _ _ _ _ _ SLOWS THINGS DOWN.

3) THE FORCE OF G _ _ _ _ _ _ PULLS OBJECTS TOWARDS THE EARTH.

Answers:1) Inertia, 2) Friction, 3) Gravity.

ELECTRICITY & MAGNETISM EXPERIMENTS

51

At the heart of every atom is an amazing secret - the power of electricity and magnetism!

BALLOON SPINNER

Why waste effort spinning balloons with your hands when all you need is magnetism!

WHAT YOU DO

1 Arrange the magnets in a line so that their ends all stick together. If the ends push apart, just turn one magnet around so that they line up.

2 One by one, take four magnets from your line without turning them and tape them to the balloon. Stick the bar magnets in a level, evenly-spaced line all the way around the balloon.

3 Tie 75 cm of string to the balloon. Ask an adult helper to press the drawing pin through the other end of the string and attach it to the top of an open door frame.

4 Take the remaining magnet and without turning it, stroke the air alongside, but not touching, one of the balloon magnets.

5 Turn your magnet so it points in the opposite direction. Repeat Step 4.

QUIZ QUESTION:

WHEN WILL YOU BE ABLE TO ROTATE THE BALLOON?

A) AT STEP 4

B) AT STEP 5

C) AT STEP 4 AND STEP 5

MAGNETS

TAPE

S   N

LINES OF FORCE

WHAT HAPPENS?

ANSWER: A

Every magnet has a north and south pole. Its magnetic field has magnetic lines of force that leave the north pole and re-enter the south pole. Opposite poles attract, but the same poles push apart.

You start the balloon with a push from your handheld magnet. The alternate pull and push on passing balloon magnets keeps the balloon turning.

WHAT YOU NEED

Balloon

String

Scissors

Measuring tape

5 bar magnets

Wide sticky tape

Drawing pin

WHAT'S NEXT?

Repeat Steps 1–3 with another balloon, but this time ensure the magnets point the opposite way to the magnets on the first balloon. What happens when you hang the two balloons together?

DID YOU KNOW?

Electric motors use magnets and electricity to produce motion.

STATIC SWINGER

You can power up this experiment using a carpet!

WHAT YOU DO

1. Wrap the foil around the thread to make a 2 cm foil ball with a 3 cm thread "tail" below the ball. Attach the other end of the thread to a table with modelling clay.

2. Rub the balloon 30 times on a woollen jumper or 20 times on a carpet.

3. Hold the balloon 1 cm from the thread tail.

WHAT YOU NEED

- 38 cm-thread
- Balloon
- Measuring tape
- Tin foil
- Scissors
- Modelling clay
- Jumper

QUIZ QUESTION:

WHAT WILL HAPPEN?

A) THE TAIL TRIES TO TOUCH THE BALLOON

B) THE BALLOON POPS!

C) THE FOIL BALL STARTS TO RISE UP THE THREAD

TABLE →

ANSWER: A

Rubbing a balloon with a woollen cloth gives the balloon an electric **charge**. The wool transfers charged particles called *electrons* to the balloon. This charge attracts uncharged objects, such as tissue paper or thread.

WHAT HAPPENS?

The tail touches the balloon, picks up charge from it and passes it to the foil. The foil now has the same type of charge as the balloon, so they repel each other.

WHAT'S NEXT?

What does the tail do after it touches the balloon?

35 CM

FOIL BALL →

1 CM

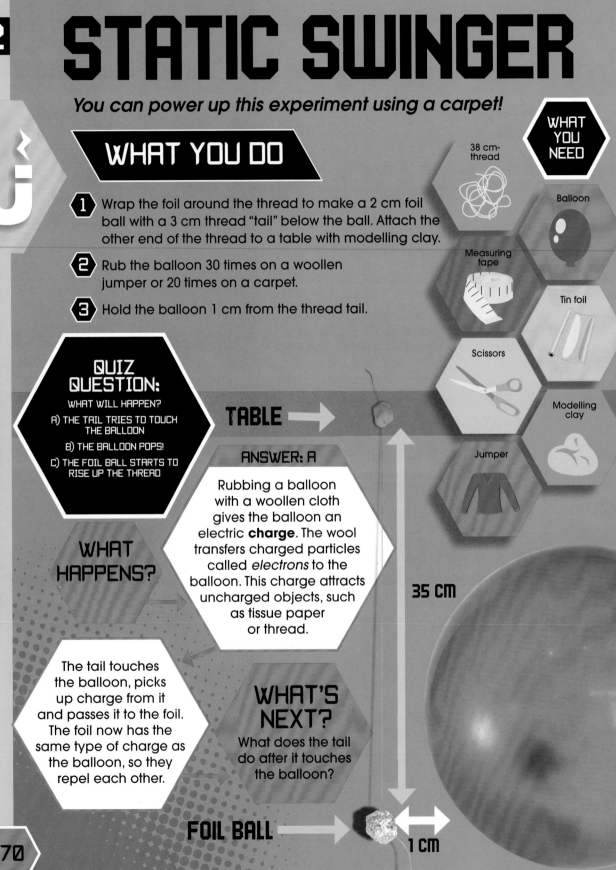

MAKE SPARKS FLY

Here's how to make your own lightning, in perfect safety!

WHAT YOU NEED

Metal spoon

Balloon

Woollen rug or blanket

WHAT YOU DO

1 Darken the room. It also needs to be a dry evening.

2 Rub the balloon on the rug or blanket 250 times firmly and very fast.

3 Put the spoon up to the balloon. You should see a tiny flash between the two. That's a spark.

QUIZ QUESTION:

WHAT CAUSES THE SPARK?

A) ELECTRONS LEAP FROM SPOON TO BALLOON

B) ELECTRONS LEAP FROM BALLOON TO SPOON

C) IT'S ELECTRICITY FROM MY BODY

WHAT HAPPENS?

ANSWER: B

The charge on the balloon cannot move until you bring a metal object close to it. The charge can jump across a small gap as a spark and travel down the metal because metals conduct electricity.

DID YOU KNOW?

When lightning strikes, electrons leap between the clouds and Earth. Lightning is over 30,000°C. The heat boosts air pressure, causing a shockwave that we hear as thunder.

ELECTRICITY & MAGNETISM EXPERIMENTS

CRAZY COMB

Combing your hair sends your electrons off on an exciting scientific journey!

WHAT YOU DO

1 Comb your hair quickly 20–30 times.

2 Collect a little honey on the back of the spoon. Trickle a thin stream of honey onto the plate.

3 Now hold the comb close to the honey stream and near the spoon.

WHAT YOU NEED

Your hair (must be clean and dry)

Small plate

Teaspoon

Honey

Clean, dry comb

WHAT HAPPENS?

QUIZ QUESTION:

WHAT WILL HAPPEN TO THE HONEY STREAM?
A) IT FORMS A SPIRAL
B) IT BENDS
C) IT STOPS AND STARTS

ANSWER: B

Combing your hair gives the comb an electric charge. This is because your hair transfers electrons to it. The charge on the comb attracts uncharged objects, such as the stream of honey.

The charge on the comb pushes electrons in the honey away and attracts the positive charge that is left.

WHAT'S NEXT?

Repeat the experiment with a thin stream of water from a tap. How do you explain your result?

MAKE A MAGNET

Don't have a magnet? That's no problem for a scientist. Here's how to make your own....

WHAT YOU NEED

- 70-80 cm of thin electrical wire
- Compass (make a compass on page 76)
- 1.5 volt battery
- Scissors
- Large steel nail or screw
- Sticky Tape

WHAT YOU DO

1 Wrap the wire around the nail many times.

2 Fasten the ends of the wire to the ends of the battery with sticky tape, making sure bare metal is touching the battery.

3 Hold the battery, nail and wire close to the compass.

QUIZ QUESTION:

WHAT WILL HAPPEN TO THE COMPASS?

A) THE COMPASS NEEDLE SWINGS AND STOPS

B) THE NEEDLE SPINS IN CIRCLES

C) THE COMPASS BEGINS TO HEAT UP

WHAT HAPPENS?

ANSWER: A

A magnetic field is a region where there is a magnetic force. A magnetic field forms around a wire when an electric current flows through it.

The battery makes the nail magnetic and they both affect the magnetic compass needle.

WHAT'S NEXT?

Can your magnetic nail pick up a paperclip?

WARNING!

IF THE BATTERY OR WIRE GETS HOT, DISCONNECT THE BATTERY RIGHT AWAY. DO NOT USE A RECHARGEABLE BATTERY FOR THIS EXPERIMENT.

ELECTRICITY & MAGNETISM EXPERIMENTS

TERRIFIC TUBE

Static electricity experiments are shockingly good fun!

WHAT YOU DO

1. Add polystyrene balls to the plastic cannister.
2. Rotate the cannister. Note how the balls fall around.
3. Rub one side of the cannister with the cotton wool hard and fast. Do this for 20 seconds.
4. Rotate the cannister again.

WHAT YOU NEED

Cotton wool

Clingfilm

Transparent plastic cannister and lid (less than 5 cm across)

Polystyrene balls less than 1 cm across

Available from craft shops – or use packing material.

WHAT HAPPENS?

QUIZ QUESTION:

WHAT WILL HAPPEN AT STEP 4?

A) SOME BALLS STICK TO ONE SIDE OF THE TUBE

B) THE INSIDE OF THE TUBE STEAMS UP

C) THE BALLS FLOAT IN MID-AIR FOR A FEW SECONDS

ANSWER: A

The cannister and polystyrene balls become **charged**.

Rubbing the cotton against the canister charges it with static electricity. The polystyrene balls inside are attracted to this charge, so they are pulled towards it.

There are two types of charges – positive charges and negative charges. Opposite charges attract each other.

So when you positively charge the canister by rubbing it with cotton, it attracts the negatively charged polystyrene balls.

CANNISTER HAS NEGATIVE CHARGE

NEGATIVE CHARGE

ELECTRONS

NEGATIVE AND POSITIVE CHARGES ATTRACT

RUB COTTON WOOL

ROTATE CANNISTER

DID YOU KNOW?

WHAT'S NEXT?

Cut a strip of clingfilm 1 cm wide and 10 cm long. Repeat Step 3 and dangle one end of the clingfilm near the cannister. What happens? What does that tell you about the clingfilm?

When charges become unbalanced on an object, they can produce sparks or shocks. A Van de Graaff generator produces so much static electricity that just touching one can make your hair stand on end!

MAKE A COMPASS

Feeling lost? Here's a science experiment to guide you home.

WHAT YOU DO

1 Stroke the pin with the magnet 50 times in the same direction. Stick the pin in the plastic bottle top with modelling clay.

2 Float the bottle top in the bowl of water and note which way the needle points.

3 Use the map to find north located at the top.

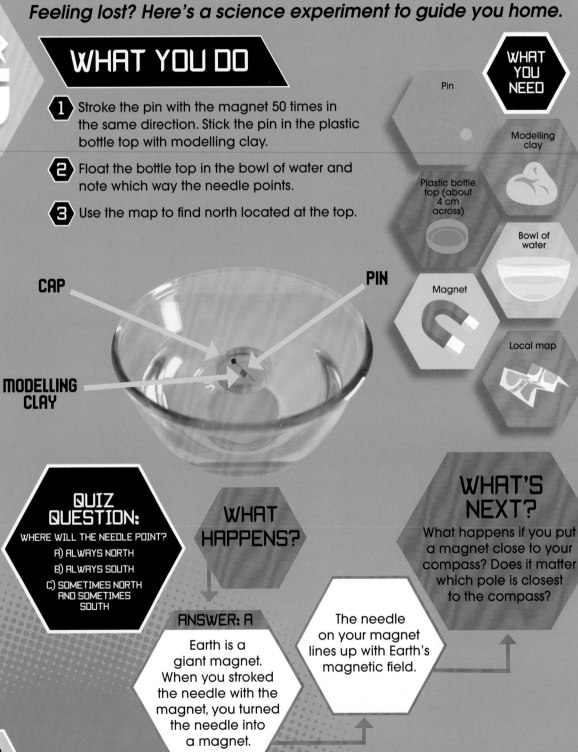

CAP

PIN

MODELLING CLAY

WHAT YOU NEED

Pin

Modelling clay

Plastic bottle top (about 4 cm across)

Bowl of water

Magnet

Local map

QUIZ QUESTION:

WHERE WILL THE NEEDLE POINT?

A) ALWAYS NORTH

B) ALWAYS SOUTH

C) SOMETIMES NORTH AND SOMETIMES SOUTH

WHAT HAPPENS?

ANSWER: A

Earth is a giant magnet. When you stroked the needle with the magnet, you turned the needle into a magnet.

The needle on your magnet lines up with Earth's magnetic field.

WHAT'S NEXT?

What happens if you put a magnet close to your compass? Does it matter which pole is closest to the compass?

WEIGHTLESS FROG

Can magnetism really make a frog float in mid-air?

WHAT YOU NEED

Pencil

Sticky Tape

2 bar magnets

Scissors

Ruler

A4 card

Coloured pencils

WHAT YOU DO

1. Draw a dotted line 1 cm from the shortest edge of the card. Draw a frog above this line, as shown. Colour it in and fold down along the dotted line so that it stands up.

2. Place the magnet on the table and put the pencil sideways on top of it. Place the other magnet on top of the pencil. Check that the magnets push each other away and then join them together with sticky tape.

3. Remove the pencil. Stand the frog on the top magnet. Your frog will now float in mid-air!

QUIZ QUESTION:

WHY DOES THE FROG APPEAR TO FLOAT?

A) THE MAGNETS REPEL EACH OTHER

B) THE FROG HAS SUPER POWERS

C) THE FROG IS LIGHTER THAN AIR

WHAT HAPPENS?

ANSWER: A

The south pole and north pole of a magnet attract each other, but two north poles and two south poles repel each other. The bottom magnet pushes the top magnet and the frog away, and that's why it appears to float.

DID YOU KNOW?

In 1997, scientists made a real frog float in a strong magnetic field. The frog was unharmed.

ELECTRICITY & MAGNETISM EXPERIMENTS

MOVING METALS

*Here's how to give a nail a makeover
and turn your money green....*

WHAT YOU DO

1. Wash and dry the coins. They must be completely dry.

2. Pour 150 ml of white vinegar into the bowl and stir in one teaspoonful of salt until it all dissolves.

3. Place the coins in the mixture. Stir the coins and leave them for 8 minutes.

4. Remove the coins with the spoon and lay them on some kitchen paper. Add a nail to the vinegar mixture.

5. Leave the nail in the mixture. Use a magnifying glass to spot tiny bubbles on the nail. After 40 minutes, remove the nail with the spoon.

ELECTRICITY & MAGNETISM EXPERIMENTS

QUIZ QUESTION:

WHAT WILL HAPPEN TO THE COINS AND NAIL?

A) THE COINS TURN BLACK AT STEP 4 AND THE NAIL TURNS SHINY AT STEP 5

B) THE COINS BEND AND THE NAIL TURNS GREEN

C) THE COINS TURN SHINY AND THE NAIL TURNS A DULL COPPER COLOUR

WHAT HAPPENS?

ANSWER: C

These chemical reactions happen because electric charges move from some atoms to others. Old copper coins are dull because they are tarnished. The acid in vinegar dissolves the tarnish, which contains copper **ions**. The copper coins come out looking newer.

The tiny bubbles contain hydrogen gas. They come from hydrogen ions in the acid.

DID YOU KNOW?

WHAT YOU NEED

12 dark copper coins

White vinegar

Measuring jug

Small bowl

Salt

Kitchen paper

2 cm iron nail or screw

Magnifying glass

Stopwatch

Plastic spoon

WHAT'S NEXT?

If you don't dry the coins, they turn turquoise-green! The color is *verdigris*. It's caused by a chemical reaction involving copper, salt, vinegar, and oxygen from the air. You can wipe away verdigris with a paper towel.

The iron nail is made from iron atoms. Electric charges move from iron atoms in the nail to the copper ions in the vinegar. The nail gets a copper coating. Electric charges also move from iron atoms to hydrogen ions in the vinegar to form gas bubbles.

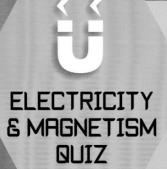

ELECTRICITY & MAGNETISM QUIZ

ADD THE MISSING WORDS:

1) ADDING ELECTRONS CREATES A _ _ _ _ _ _ _ _ CHARGE.

2) FEWER ELECTRONS CREATES A _ _ _ _ _ _ _ _ CHARGE.

3) AN AREA OF MAGNETIC FORCE IS CALLED A MAGNETIC _ _ _ _ _.

79

Answers:1) Negative, 2) Positive, 3) Field.

Light is mysterious – sparkling, colourful and always amazing. In the next few pages you'll be making reflections, rainbows and even ghosts!

TURN LIGHT ON ITS HEAD

Turn the world upside-down without standing on your head! All it takes is a little light science.

WHAT YOU DO

1 Ask an adult to make a tiny hole no bigger than 0.2 cm in the centre of the end of the tube.

2 Roll the black paper into the cardboard tube so that it fits tightly inside. Secure the paper in place with sticky tape.

3 Cut out a circle of greaseproof paper the same size as the end of the tube. Tape the paper over the end of the tube. Make sure the paper circle fits tightly over the tube.

4 Pull the coat over your head. Stick the tube through the gap in the coat (with the greaseproof paper circle inside of the coat) and look at an object. Look at the greaseproof paper circle (but not too closely).

GREASEPROOF PAPER

STICKY TAPE

QUIZ QUESTION:

WHAT MAKES THE IMAGE UPSIDE-DOWN?

A) THE GREASEPROOF PAPER

B) THE LIGHT

C) MY BRAIN

UPSIDE-DOWN IMAGE

LIGHT CROSSES OVER

WHAT HAPPENS?

ANSWER: B
Light from the outside travels through the tiny hole in your tube, crosses over and shows a projected upside-down image on the greaseproof paper.

The image is dim because the small hole only lets a little light through. You need to be in the dark to see the dim image.

WHAT'S NEXT?

Your tube is a simple camera obscura. It's the most basic form of lens, and works a lot like your own eye (see page 93)!

LENS

UPSIDE-DOWN IMAGE OF OBJECT

OBJECT

WHAT YOU NEED

Black coat

Black paper or card

Greaseproof paper

Sticky tape

Bright sunny day

A cardboard tube with a metal or cardboard end

DID YOU KNOW?

Many famous artists used a camera obscura to help them paint scenery. It led to the invention of photography and the first camera.

LIGHT TRAVELS IN STRAIGHT LINES

MAKE A SUNSET

Sunsets can be very beautiful, and now you can make your own with this experiment.

WHAT YOU DO

1 Add half a teaspoon of milk to the water and stir well.

2 Close the curtains in the room and turn off the lights. The experiment works best when it's dark.

3 Shine the torch through the glass of milk. Look at the side of the glass (at a 90° angle from the light beam).

4 Now shine the torch through the glass of milk and look at the milk from the opposite side of the glass.

WHAT YOU NEED

Small torch (not LED)

Tall glass of water

Teaspoon

Full-fat milk

Milk

Blue and red tissue paper

QUIZ QUESTION:

WHAT WILL HAPPEN?

A) THE MIXTURE WILL BE SLIGHTLY BLUE AT STEP 3 AND SLIGHTLY RED AT STEP 4

B) IT'S THE OTHER WAY AROUND

C) THE MIXTURE WILL TURN A SICKLY PALE GREEN AT STEPS 3 AND 4

WHAT HAPPENS?

ANSWER: A

Light waves from a torch pass straight through pure water but the fat droplets in milk "scatter" light waves.

Blue light scatters more, becoming trapped in the milk, so the milk looks slightly blue when looked at from the side. The longer red light waves make their way through the milk because they scatter less.

LONGER WAVES = RED

SHORTER WAVES = BLUE

WHAT'S NEXT?

Does your experiment explain why sunrises and sunsets are red? Now try shining the light through blue or red tissue paper. What happens?

RED LIGHT SCATTERS LESS

BLUE LIGHT SCATTERS MORE

LIGHT FLOW

You might think light moves in a straight line, but you can actually pour it like water!

WHAT YOU NEED

- Small torch
- 2-litre empty plastic bottle
- Black paper or card
- Scissors
- Sticky Tape
- Marker pen
- Ruler

WHAT YOU DO

1. Trim 4 cm from the end of the paper or card and wrap the rest around the lower part of the bottle. Secure with sticky tape.

2. Make a 5-8 mm hole with the scissor point through the paper and bottle as shown. Slightly enlarge the hole in the paper only.

3. Hold the bottle up to the light and mark the side opposite the hole. Make a small hole in the paper where the mark is located.

4. Fill the bottle with water over a bathtub and replace the top. Turn off the light – have an adult help you see what you're doing. Remove the top and place your torch against the small hole in the paper.

WATER STREAM

5 CM

LIGHT EXPERIMENTS

QUIZ QUESTION:

WHY WILL THE STREAM BE SHINING?

A) IT DRAWS LIGHT FROM THE BOTTLE

B) LIGHT REFLECTS INSIDE THE STREAM

C) THE STREAM'S MOVEMENT ENERGY BRIGHTENS LIGHT

ANSWER: B

The angle of the light relative to the stream stops light escaping. The light reflects back and forth inside the stream.

WHAT HAPPENS?

DID YOU KNOW?

Light signals reflect inside an optical fibre cable in the same way as your experiment. These cables carry telephone and broadband signals.

LOOK BEHIND YOU

This simple experiment lets you see what's going on behind you...

WHAT YOU DO

1 Cut out a piece of shiny card 30 cm long and 9 cm wide. If you don't have shiny card, staple smooth tin foil to paper this size.

2 Close the curtains in the room and turn on the light.

3 Bend the card and hold it in front of your face. Stand with your back to the light. Can you see the light in the card?

WHAT YOU NEED

Ruler

Pencil

Scissors

Shiny card

QUIZ QUESTION:

WHY BEND THE CARD IN FRONT OF YOUR FACE?

A) TO KEEP MY FACE COOL

B) TO KEEP LIGHT OUT OF MY EYES

C) TO REFLECT LIGHT INTO MY EYES

DID YOU KNOW?

Car wing mirrors work in much the same way. What you see depends on the angle of the mirror.

WHAT HAPPENS?

ANSWER: C

Light travels in straight lines. Shiny surfaces reflect light. The angle of the card changes the angle that light is reflected.

MAKE AN ECLIPSE

Every so often the moon puts Earth in the shade. Here's how that works...

WHAT YOU NEED

- Table tennis ball (or similar)
- Lid or bottle top
- Tennis ball (or similar)
- Measuring tape
- Torch
- Table

WHAT YOU DO

1. Set up the experiment as shown below.
2. Darken the room – the experiment works best at night.
3. Hold the torch 60 cm from the table tennis ball. Look for the shadow of the smaller ball on the larger ball.

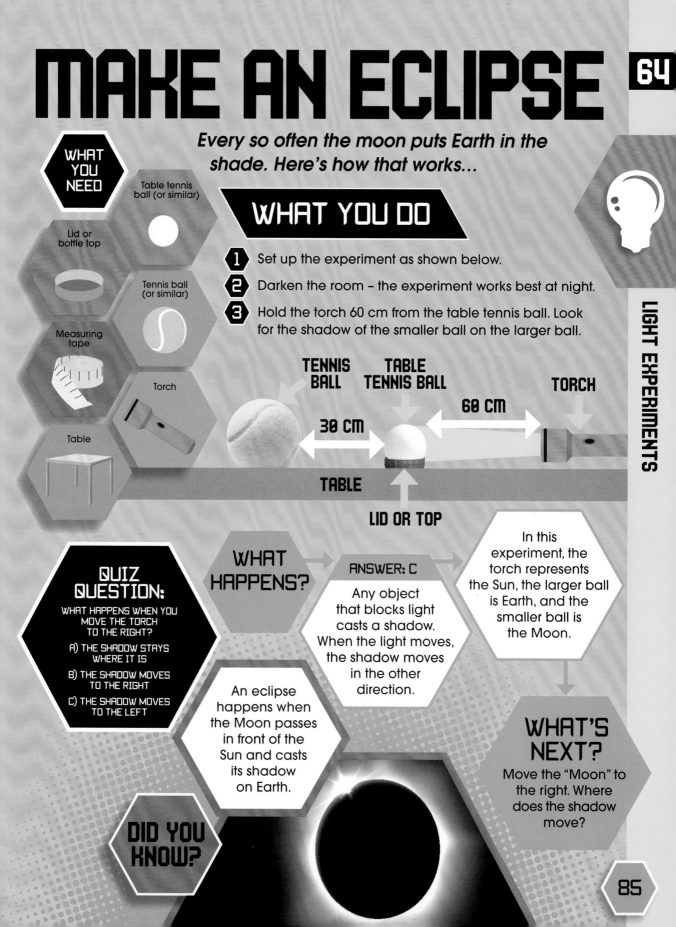

TENNIS BALL

TABLE TENNIS BALL

TORCH

60 CM

30 CM

TABLE

LID OR TOP

QUIZ QUESTION:

WHAT HAPPENS WHEN YOU MOVE THE TORCH TO THE RIGHT?

A) THE SHADOW STAYS WHERE IT IS

B) THE SHADOW MOVES TO THE RIGHT

C) THE SHADOW MOVES TO THE LEFT

WHAT HAPPENS?

ANSWER: C

Any object that blocks light casts a shadow. When the light moves, the shadow moves in the other direction.

In this experiment, the torch represents the Sun, the larger ball is Earth, and the smaller ball is the Moon.

An eclipse happens when the Moon passes in front of the Sun and casts its shadow on Earth.

WHAT'S NEXT?

Move the "Moon" to the right. Where does the shadow move?

DID YOU KNOW?

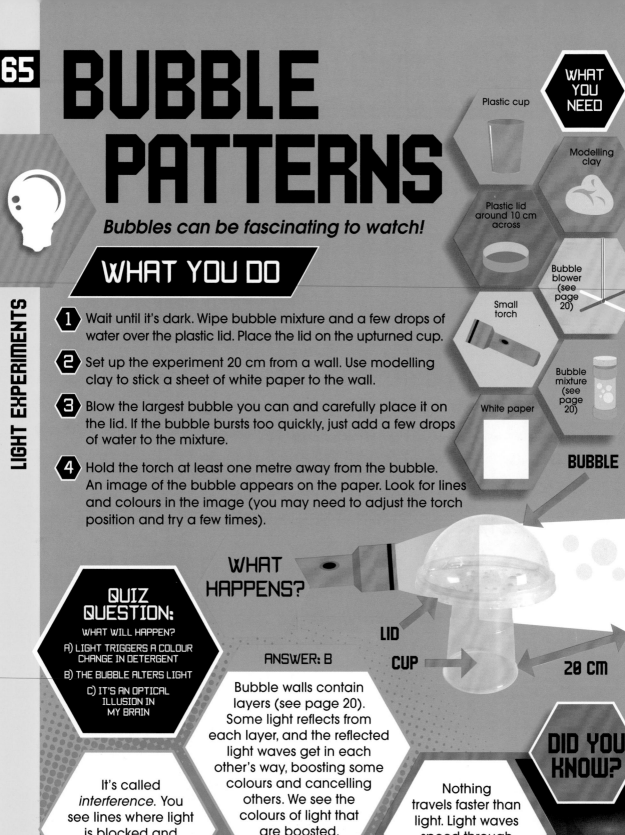

BUBBLE PATTERNS

Bubbles can be fascinating to watch!

WHAT YOU NEED

Plastic cup

Modelling clay

Plastic lid around 10 cm across

Bubble blower (see page 20)

Small torch

Bubble mixture (see page 20)

White paper

BUBBLE

WHAT YOU DO

1 Wait until it's dark. Wipe bubble mixture and a few drops of water over the plastic lid. Place the lid on the upturned cup.

2 Set up the experiment 20 cm from a wall. Use modelling clay to stick a sheet of white paper to the wall.

3 Blow the largest bubble you can and carefully place it on the lid. If the bubble bursts too quickly, just add a few drops of water to the mixture.

4 Hold the torch at least one metre away from the bubble. An image of the bubble appears on the paper. Look for lines and colours in the image (you may need to adjust the torch position and try a few times).

WHAT HAPPENS?

LID

CUP

20 CM

QUIZ QUESTION:

WHAT WILL HAPPEN?

A) LIGHT TRIGGERS A COLOUR CHANGE IN DETERGENT

B) THE BUBBLE ALTERS LIGHT

C) IT'S AN OPTICAL ILLUSION IN MY BRAIN

ANSWER: B

Bubble walls contain layers (see page 20). Some light reflects from each layer, and the reflected light waves get in each other's way, boosting some colours and cancelling others. We see the colours of light that are boosted.

It's called *interference*. You see lines where light is blocked and colours where light waves are boosted.

DID YOU KNOW?

Nothing travels faster than light. Light waves speed through space at almost 300,000 km per second!

MAKE A RAINBOW

You never know when a rainbow will appear, so here's how to make your very own.

WHAT YOU NEED

Bright sunny day (or a small torch after dark)

CD

White paper

WHAT YOU DO

1 Place the paper in a dark corner of a room or at the bottom of an open box. If you use a torch, make sure to place the paper in front of the torch.

2 Hold the CD with the shiny side up. Tilt the CD at different angles to reflect light onto the paper.

LIGHT EXPERIMENTS

QUIZ QUESTION:

WHAT WILL YOU SEE?
A) RAINBOW COLOURS
B) BLACK-AND-WHITE PATTERNS
C) FLASHING DOTS AND DASHES

WHAT HAPPENS?

ANSWER: A

A CD reflects light in a different way from a bubble. The data lines in the CD form ridges. Light reflects from the different ridges, producing interference patterns we see as rainbow colours.

To see the lines caused by interference, try tilting the CD at different angles.

DID YOU KNOW?

You can see similar colours in an oil spill because a thin layer of oil causes similar light interference.

WHAT'S NEXT?

Try shining a bright LED, long-life, or filament bulb at the CD. How are the colours different with another bulb?

MAKE WATER COLOURFUL

Even water that appears to be clear can actually be surprisingly colourful....

WHAT YOU DO

1 Place the glass inside the coloured mug.

2 Fill the glass with water to 1.5 cm above the top of the mug.

3 Now, holding the glass by the rim in one hand and the mug in the other, raise and lower the glass and look at the water from different angles.

RAISE AND LOWER THE GLASS

QUIZ QUESTION:

WHAT DO YOU NOTICE ABOUT THE COLOUR OF THE WATER?

A) IT'S MOSTLY THE COLOUR OF THE MUG

B) IT'S THE SAME AS ALWAYS

C) IT SEEMS BRIGHTER

WHAT HAPPENS?

ANSWER: A

An object's colour depends on the light waves that reflect off it. For example, blue objects reflect light waves that make blue light.

In this experiment, the mug's reflected light waves reflect a second time inside the glass. It looks as if the water is coloured.

WHAT'S NEXT?

Why does the colour change when you alter the water level?

TURN ONE TOY INTO A CROWD

One toy not enough for you? Then try this experiment to make lots more!

WHAT YOU NEED

- 2 mirrors (one small enough to hold safely)
- Toy figure
- Torch

WHAT YOU DO

1. Place the figure a few centimetres in front of one mirror.

2. Hold the second mirror 20 cm in front of the first and peer over it to see many toys as the reflection bounces between the mirrors.

WHAT HAPPENS?

ANSWER: A

Mirror atoms absorb some light waves with every reflection. The more times an image is reflected, the dimmer it appears.

QUIZ QUESTION:

WHY WILL THE REFLECTIONS GET DIMMER?

A) NOT ALL LIGHT WAVES ARE REFLECTED

B) LIGHT WAVES LOSE ENERGY AS THEY REFLECT

C) DARKER REFLECTIONS COME FROM THE BACK OF THE MIRROR

MIRROR 2

WHAT'S NEXT?

Does it help if you shine a light on the figure? Why?

MIRROR 1

WARNING!

DON'T TRY TO LIFT OR MOVE LARGE MIRRORS!

20 CM

MAKE A GHOST

Scientists don't believe in ghosts, but they do believe in this one. It's a science ghost!

WHAT YOU DO

1 Cut one side of the box off as shown and fold it out.

2 Cut an opening in the box a little smaller than your piece of cellophane. Tape the cellophane over this area.

3 Place the figure in the box facing the cellophane. Wait for dark or darken the room and shine the torch from above and behind the figure. A ghostly figure appears reflected in the cellophane to the left of the box. If necessary, adjust the position of the figure and torch until you see the "ghost."

❶

FOLD

CUT

❷

CUT

❸

QUIZ QUESTION:

WHY WAIT UNTIL DARK?

A) IT'S SCARIER AFTER DARK

B) THE FIGURE IS SEE-THROUGH AGAINST A DARK BACKGROUND

C) THE FIGURE IS MORE VISIBLE AGAINST A DARK BACKGROUND

WHAT HAPPENS?

ANSWER: C

Imagine looking out of a window at night. When the room is lit, you can see your reflection. Your reflection is there in the day, but you can't make it out because of the light coming through the window.

WHAT YOU NEED

Small torch

A toy figure

Cardboard box

Stiff cellophane from packaging

Scissors

Sticky Tape

Cloth

WHAT'S NEXT?

Shine the torch behind the cellophane. Cover the torch with cloth and shine it on the figure. Why is it harder to see the figure in both cases?

DID YOU KNOW?

Your ghost experiment is a theatre illusion called Pepper's Ghost. Mr. Pepper was a Victorian scientist who helped to invent the trick.

LIGHT QUIZ

THE MISSING WORD IS EITHER BLUE OR RED:

1) BLUE OBJECTS REFLECT LIGHT WAVES THAT MAKE ____ LIGHT.

2) ___ LIGHT HAS LONGER WAVES THAN ____ WAVES.

3) ___ LIGHT SCATTERS LESS THAN ____ LIGHT.

Answers:1) Blue, 2) Red, Blue 3) Red, Blue.

The human body is an incredible piece of science. These fun experiments will show you just how amazing it is....

MAKE A MODEL EYEBALL

Did you know there's more to your vision than meets the eye?

WHAT YOU DO

1 Cut a piece of card 5 cm long and 1 cm wide. Using the ruler, draw a line across the middle of the card and colour one half blue and the other half red.

2 Set up the experiment as shown below.

3 Wet the bubble blower and plastic lid.

4 Blow the largest bubble you can and carefully place it on the lid. If the bubble bursts too soon, add a few drops of water to the mixture and try again.

5 Hold your card vertically, with one colour on top about 15 cm to the side of the bubble.

6 Shine your torch at the card and look at the reflections in the bubble.

QUIZ QUESTION:

WHAT WILL YOU SEE?

A) TWO REFLECTIONS – THE ONE NEAREST THE CARD IS THE RIGHT WAY UP. THE ONE ON THE OPPOSITE SIDE OF THE BUBBLE IS UPSIDE DOWN

B) JUST LIKE A) BUT BOTH REFLECTIONS ARE UPSIDE DOWN

C) JUST LIKE A) BUT THE COLOURS HAVE CHANGED – THE RED IS YELLOW AND THE BLUE IS GREEN

CARD

LID

CUP

15 CM

WHAT HAPPENS?

ANSWER: A

The lens in your eyeball bends light entering your pupil so that an upside-down and reversed image is projected onto your retina.

The curved surface of the bubble bends light like your curved lens to produce an upside-down and reversed image on the back wall of the bubble.

WHAT YOU NEED

Bubble mixture (see page 20)

Bubble blower (see page 20)

Scissors

Small torch

Red and blue felt-tip pens

Card

Plastic cup

Ruler

Plastic lid

Pencil

RETINA

LENS

PUPIL

NERVE

DID YOU KNOW?

Your retina sends the image to your brain as nerve signals, and your clever brain turns the image the right way up and the right way around.

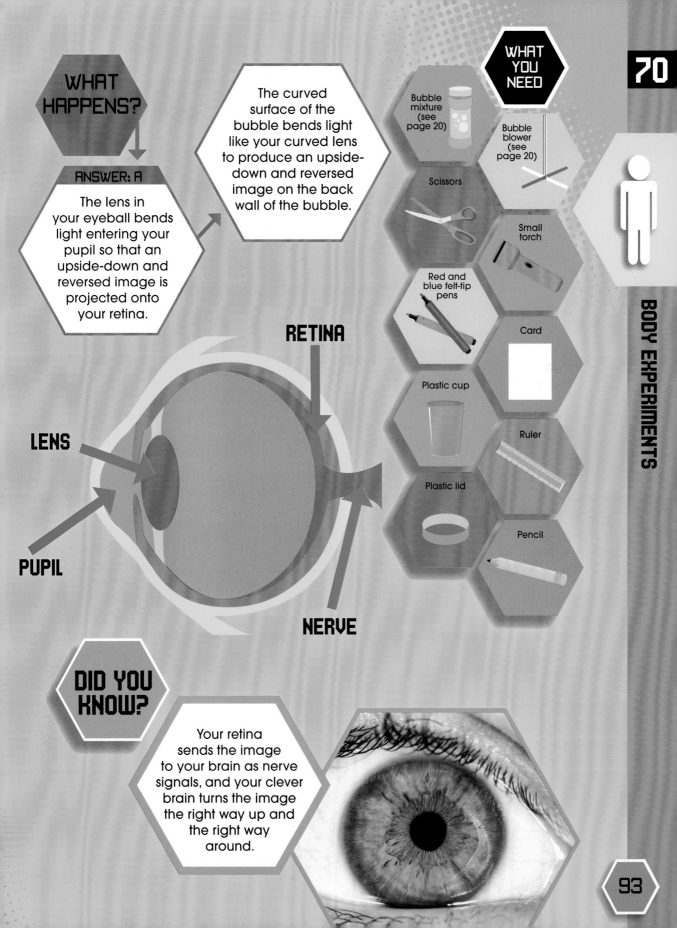

TEST YOUR CO-ORDINATION

It's sometimes hard to do two things at once. But don't worry, it's all in the mind!

WHAT YOU DO

1 Sit on a chair and cross your legs.

2 Lift your right leg and rotate your right foot in a clockwise direction. If you're left-handed, rotate your left foot instead.

3 Now try to write a number '6' on paper at the same time.

WHAT YOU NEED

Paper

Chair

Pencil

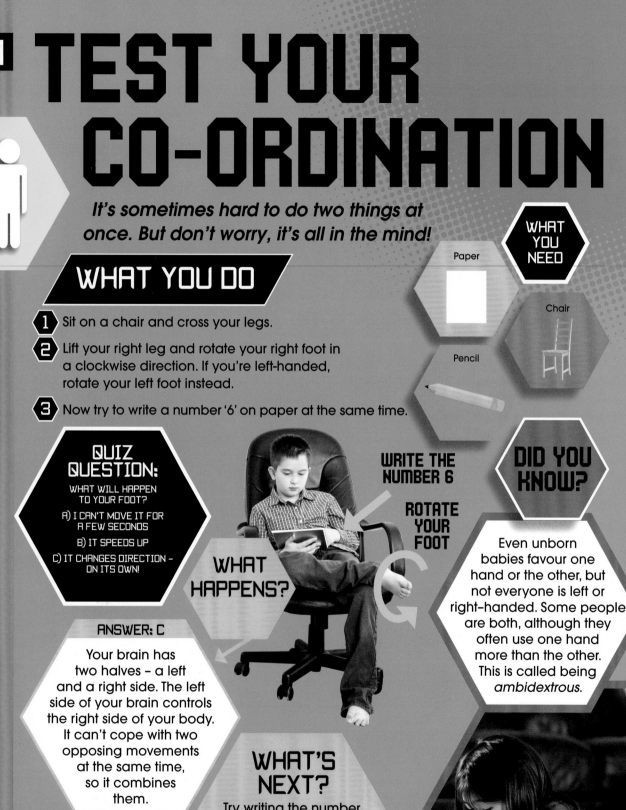

WRITE THE NUMBER 6

ROTATE YOUR FOOT

QUIZ QUESTION:

WHAT WILL HAPPEN TO YOUR FOOT?

A) I CAN'T MOVE IT FOR A FEW SECONDS

B) IT SPEEDS UP

C) IT CHANGES DIRECTION – ON ITS OWN!

WHAT HAPPENS?

ANSWER: C

Your brain has two halves – a left and a right side. The left side of your brain controls the right side of your body. It can't cope with two opposing movements at the same time, so it combines them.

WHAT'S NEXT?

Try writing the number '6' with your other hand. Now try writing '6' the wrong way around. Why could these methods help?

DID YOU KNOW?

Even unborn babies favour one hand or the other, but not everyone is left or right-handed. Some people are both, although they often use one hand more than the other. This is called being *ambidextrous*.

TEST YOUR STRENGTH

Put your muscles to the ultimate test.

WHAT YOU NEED

Paper

A pair of weighing scales (not digital)

Pencil

A friend or adult helper

WHAT YOU DO

1 Hold the weighing scales on their side between your hands and then push as hard as you can. Note the number shown on the dial.

2 Lie on your back on the floor as shown below, with your feet against a wall. Fold your arms behind your head and rest your head on your hands. Ask a friend or adult to put the scales underneath your feet.

3 Push as hard as you can on the scales. Use your arms to stop your head being pushed backwards. Record the number shown on the dial.

WHAT HAPPENS?

ANSWER: B

This experiment tests your arm's biceps and the extensor muscles in your legs. The leg muscles are larger, so they should be stronger. The higher the number on the scales, the greater force is being exerted on it.

QUIZ QUESTION:

WHEN WILL YOU BE ABLE TO PUSH HARDEST?

A) STEP 1

B) STEP 3

C) THEY'RE ABOUT EQUAL

WHAT'S NEXT?

Try Step 1 with the dial on the scales facing right and then left. Do your results differ? If you're right handed, your right arm is usually stronger than your left arm.

SCALE

PUSH

PUSH   SCALE

FOOTPRINTS

Your footprints leave a trail of science!

WHAT YOU DO

1 Walk 5 metres along the beach barefoot. If you're not near a beach, try to find a sandpit in a playground. Notice the shape of your footprints in the sand.

2 Measure the distance between the footprints of your left foot and right foot.

3 Stand more than 10 metres behind your starting point in Step 1, then run alongside your walking footprints. Notice the shape of your footprints.

WHAT YOU NEED

A beach with firm damp sand or a sandpit

Tape measure

BALL

QUIZ QUESTION:

HOW DO YOU EXPLAIN DIFFERENT-SHAPED FOOTPRINTS AT STEP 2 AND 3?

A) I RUN MORE ON THE FRONT PART OF MY FOOT

B) I RUN MORE ON THE BACK PART OF MY FOOT

C) MY FOOT SPREADS SLIGHTLY WHEN I RUN

WHAT HAPPENS?

ANSWER: A

When we walk barefoot, we usually walk on the heels and balls of our feet or the whole foot. You should see whole footprints at Step 2. Most people run on the front of their bare feet.

WHAT'S NEXT?

Compare the distance between your walking and running footprints. How do you explain the difference?

HEEL

MAKE A LUNG

Discover how you breathe with this experiment.

WHAT YOU NEED

Large balloon

2-litre plastic bottle

Plastic funnel

Tape measure

WHAT YOU DO

1 Blow up and let the air out of the balloon three times or until the balloon is saggy.

2 Roll the balloon 2 cm over the neck of the funnel.

3 Push the balloon and funnel neck into the bottle. Make sure it fits tightly.

4 Now squeeze the bottle.

WHAT HAPPENS?

QUIZ QUESTION:

WHAT WILL HAPPEN TO THE BALLOON?

A) IT FILLS WITH AIR

B) THE AIR IS FORCED OUT OF IT

C) IT GLUES ITSELF TO THE SIDE OF THE BOTTLE

ANSWER: B

Squeezing the bottle forces air into a smaller area. Air pressure inside the bottle increases and forces air from the balloon. When you release the bottle, air pressure drops and air flows into the balloon.

You breathe in a similar way. As your chest expands, your lungs expand too and air flows in. As your chest reduces in size, air is pushed from your lungs.

WHAT'S NEXT?

Ask a friend to measure around your chest when you breathe in and out. Is there a difference?

FUNNEL

BALLOON

TEST YOUR SENSE OF BALANCE

Balancing is harder than you think!

WHAT YOU DO

1 Open the door halfway and stand with your nose pressed against the edge of the door.

2 Now try to stand on your tiptoes.

WHAT YOU NEED

Door

QUIZ QUESTION:

WHAT WILL HAPPEN?

A) IT'S EASY!

B) IT'S POSSIBLE IF YOU STICK YOUR ARMS OUT SIDEWAYS

C) IT'S IMPOSSIBLE

SEMI-CIRCULAR CANALS

WHAT HAPPENS?

ANSWER: C

We balance our body mass around a point called 'the centre of gravity'. If the centre is too far in one direction, we are unbalanced and fall over.

To stand on your tiptoes, you lean your centre of gravity forwards. But you can't do that here because the door is in the way.

WHAT'S NEXT?

Try standing on one leg. Now try this with your eyes closed. Is vision important in balancing?

DID YOU KNOW?

Our inner ears contain structures called *semi-circular canals*. These fluid-filled tubes contain sensory hairs that detect movements as the head turns. Nearby structures detect changes in the speed your head is moving. Balance is maintained through the ears, eyes and sensory systems.

FOOL YOUR BRAIN

If your brain's so clever, why is it so easy to fool?

WHAT YOU NEED

2 coins (of the same type)

Small torch

White paper

WHAT YOU DO

1 Wait until dark. Switch off all lights and hold the torch at arm's length. Move it rapidly in circles, watching what happens to the light.

2 For the next experiment, switch off the torch. Hold the coins between your fingers with the paper in the background. Rub the coins rapidly up and down.

BODY EXPERIMENTS

QUIZ QUESTION:

WHAT WILL YOU SEE?

A) SCARY SHADOWS AT STEP 1 AND A COIN VANISHES AT STEP 2

B) LIGHT STREAKS AND CIRCLES AT STEP 1 AND AN EXTRA COIN AT STEP 2

C) THE LIGHT TURNS PINK AT STEP 1 AND THE COINS GROW LARGER AT STEP 2

WHAT HAPPENS?

ANSWER: B

When you see something, your brain briefly stores the image. Your brain combines images if you see them in quick succession.

This is why you see the light as a continuous streak or circle and why you see the coin in two places at once.

DID YOU KNOW?

This also explains why you can see films as a moving picture. They're made up of thousands of pictures shown very fast.

GROW A STICK PERSON

Stick people are lines on paper. They're not actually real or alive. So why does your brain think they are?

WHAT YOU NEED

White paper

Clingfilm

Ruler

Black felt-tip pen

Scissors

Paperclips

WHAT YOU DO

1 Draw lines on the paper as shown.

2 Cut out two clingfilm pieces and draw your stick figures. Check that your figures are exactly the same size.

3 CM

3 CM

1 CM   1 CM

3 Place the figures on the lines as shown. Now move the second figure towards the first.

QUIZ QUESTION:

WHAT DO YOU NOTICE?

A) THE LEFT FIGURE IS GROWING

B) THE RIGHT FIGURE IS GROWING

C) BOTH FIGURES ARE GROWING!

WHAT HAPPENS?

ANSWER: B

No-one is sure why the right figure appears to grow. Perhaps your brain views the lines like a 3-D scene. It thinks the figure on the left is smaller because it appears more distant.

WHAT'S NEXT?

Repeat the experiment with paperclips instead of stick people. Do you still get the same results?

DID YOU KNOW?

Your brain also gets fooled when the Moon is close to the horizon. You think the Moon is larger than it really it is.

TAKE YOUR FINGERPRINTS

Could you be a science crime buster? Find out now as you discover what makes fingerprints really special!

WHAT YOU NEED

- Magnifying glass
- 2 sheets of white paper
- Pencil
- Scissors
- Sticky Tape

WHAT YOU DO

1 Rub the pencil on the sheet of paper to make a thick mark that's larger than your fingertip.

2 Now rub your finger on your forehead and press it firmly onto the mark.

3 Press your fingertip on to the sticky side of a piece of tape. After a few seconds, remove your finger from the tape.

4 Stick the tape onto the second sheet of paper. Examine the fingerprint using a magnifying glass under bright light.

WHAT HAPPENS?

ANSWER: A

Oil will help you see the pattern of your fingerprint.

QUIZ QUESTION:

WHY DO YOU NEED TO RUB YOUR FOREHEAD?

A) TO MAKE MY FINGER OILY

B) TO MAKE BIGGER FINGERPRINTS

C) TO THINK BETTER

WHAT'S NEXT?

Try taking someone else's prints. Can you spot any differences?

DID YOU KNOW?

To prevent election fraud in some countries, voters have a semi-permanent ink applied to their fingers. The ink stays on their fingers for up to 4 weeks.

TEST YOUR EARS

Ears are great for hearing, but even ears have their limits....

WHAT YOU DO

1 It's best to try this experiment outside in the garden or in a large empty room. If you're inside, ask an adult if you can use chalk on the floor. Tune the radio to a talk station.

2 Draw a chalk circle 4 metres around the chair.

3 Sit on the chair, close your eyes and stick your fingers in your ears. Friend 1 tiptoes around the circle holding the radio, which is switched off.

4 Friend 1 switches on the radio with the sound fairly low, and Friend 2 taps you on the shoulder. Take your hands from your ears and point to where you think the sound comes from. Friend 2 marks the direction in chalk.

5 Repeat Steps 3 and 4 with a finger in one ear.

QUIZ QUESTION:

WHAT WILL YOU FIND OUT?
A) STEP 5 WAS HARDER THAN 4
B) STEP 4 WAS HARDER THAN 5
C) BOTH STEPS WERE EASY!

FINGER IN EAR

RADIO

8 METRES

WHAT HAPPENS?

ANSWER: A

Remember the 'Did You Know?' fact on page 55? Having two ears helps you judge sound direction. Your brain distinguishes tiny sound and time differences between the signals from each ear. It's harder if one ear is blocked.

WHAT'S NEXT?

Test your friends. Measure the angle between where they point and the radio's position.

WHAT YOU NEED

Radio

Chair

Measuring tape

Chalk

Two friends (Friend 1 and Friend 2)

DID YOU KNOW?

Your ears contain the smallest bone in your body. The *stapes* is one of three bones that pass on sound vibrations in your middle ear. It's less than 3 mm long!

STAPES

BODY QUIZ

WHICH OF THESE BODY PARTS...

1) MOVES YOUR ARM?
2) CONTROLS THE LEFT SIDE OF YOUR BODY?
3) HELP YOU TO SEE?

A LEFT BRAIN   **B** BICEPS   **C** SHOULDER

D RIGHT BRAIN   **E** RETINA   **F** EYEBROWS

Answers:1) B, 2) D, 3) E.

Planet Earth is alive with all sorts of living things. In this chapter, you'll get to know just a few of them....

VENUS FLYTRAP GAME

What do we know about one of the strangest plants on the planet?

WHAT YOU DO

1. Measure the length and width of your hand. Use these measurements to draw an oval on the red paper. Cut this shape out. It should be a little larger than your hand.

2. Lay the red shape on the green paper and trace around it, making a larger oval. Draw 'teeth' around the outline and then cut out the shape.

3. Lay the red shape on the green shape and staple them together. Fold both shapes in half. You've now made your model Venus flytrap's mouth.

4. Open the shape out and lay it on a table, green side facing up. Put a green glove on your hand and lay that hand on the shape with your fingers together. Ask a friend to stick your fingers to one half of the shape with tape. Use your other hand to fold down the 'jaws' of the shape.

5. Hold your hand and the shape partly unfolded. Look away and ask your friend to touch the shape over your fingers with the pencil. Try to quickly close the mouth around the pencil.

WHAT YOU NEED

- Friend
- A4 red paper
- Green gloves (not vital)
- A4 green paper
- Pencil
- Scissors
- Ruler
- Stapler
- Wide sticky tape

FOLD

CUT

QUIZ QUESTION:

WHY DO VENUS FLYTRAPS HAVE 'JAWS'?

A) TO ALLOW LITTLE BUGS TO ESCAPE

B) TO BITE BUGS IN HALF

C) TO STOP BUGS FROM ESCAPING BEFORE THE LEAF CLOSES

WHAT HAPPENS?

ANSWER: C

The leaf has trigger hairs near the bottom. If these are bent, it triggers the leaf to close, trapping insects.

DID YOU KNOW?

Venus flytraps only grow in marshy parts of South Eastern USA. The trap closes when a bug (usually an ant or spider) touches its trigger hairs. The leaf shuts in a fraction of a second!

MAKE YOUR OWN SEED SPINNERS

Engineers have studied spinning seeds to help them design aircraft! Experiment with seed spinners to design your own super spinner.

WHAT YOU DO

PENCIL LINE

3 CM

1. Draw a straight line across the A4 paper, around 3 cm from the bottom.

2. Cut out the strip and find the centre of it. Make a pencil mark 3 cm to the left of this. Draw a line from the bottom to the top of the strip, stopping halfway.

3. Make a pencil mark 3 cm to the right of the centre. This time, draw a line from the top to the bottom of the strip, stopping halfway.

4. Cut along the lines.

5. Bend and twist the strip, to push the cut paper together. You have created the two wings of your spinner.

BEND AND TWIST

6. Stick a small ball of modelling clay at the base of the loop. This is the seed.

7. Go outside (or inside and carefully stand on a chair) and ask an adult to help you to find a safe place to drop the seed spinner from a height. Watch it spin as it falls to the floor. Measure the distance it falls from your feet.

MODELLING CLAY

QUIZ QUESTION:

WHAT WILL HAPPEN?

A) THE SPINNER FALLS DOWN AND AWAY FROM YOU

B) THE SPINNER FLIES OFF LIKE A HELICOPTER

C) THE SPINNER FALLS APART

WHAT HAPPENS?

ANSWER: A

Plants need to spread their seeds as far as possible, so they don't all start growing in the same place. Some tree seeds spin like this as they fall to the ground. This keeps them in the air longer, making it more likely that a gust of wind will blow them away from the tree.

WHAT YOU NEED

Paper

Pencil and ruler

Scissors

Modelling clay

WHAT'S NEXT?

Try making a spinner with longer or shorter wings by making pencil marks closer to or further from the centre of the strip. Which spinner stays in the air longest? You could try making them with different types of paper, different-shaped wings, or heavier seeds. Remember to change just one thing at a time, or it will not be a fair test.

DID YOU KNOW?

These humble spinning seeds have actually helped improve technologies of planetary probes to slow down their descent and explore the atmosphere of planets such as Mars.

SEE LIKE A CHAMELEON

Now you can see eye-to-eye with a lizard.

WHAT YOU DO

1. Cut out two egg holders from the egg box.
2. Use the pen to make off-centre holes in each holder.
3. Hold the egg holders over your eyes. You can now see in two different directions.

WHAT YOU NEED

Egg box

Scissors

Pen

QUIZ QUESTION:

WHY IS THIS USEFUL FOR A CHAMELEON?

A) THEY CAN CATCH INSECTS MORE EASILY

B) THEY CAN SPOT DANGER FROM TWO DIRECTIONS

C) IT'S A PARTY TRICK TO IMPRESS OTHER CHAMELEONS!

ANSWER: A

When a chameleon spots an insect to eat, it swivels its eyes to face the bug. Using both eyes enables it to judge distance. Then it shoots out its tongue to grab its victim.

WHAT HAPPENS?

DID YOU KNOW?

Snakes and monkeys eat chameleons, so they have to watch out for danger at all times.

MAKE MICROBE FIZZ

They may be impossible to see with the naked eye, but microbes are everywhere!

WHAT YOU NEED

- Dry yeast
- Funnel
- Teaspoon
- Sugar
- Saucepan with lid
- Sieve
- Measuring jug
- Ground ginger
- Tablespoon
- 500-ml plastic bottle
- Lemon juice

WARNING!
DO NOT LEAVE IN THE FRIDGE FOR MORE THAN 36 HOURS. DO NOT DRINK THE EXPERIMENT!

WHAT YOU DO

1. Ask an adult to boil 500 ml of water in the saucepan. Stir in one-third of a tablespoon of ground ginger, 70 g of sugar and one tablespoon of lemon juice.

2. Cover the pan and leave on the heat until the mixture is warm.

3. Stir in one-third of a teaspoon of yeast. Replace the lid and leave for two hours with the heat off.

4. Sift the mixture into the jug. Using the funnel, pour the liquid into the bottle until it's 4 cm from the top. Screw the top tightly onto the bottle.

5. Leave in the fridge for at least twelve hours. When you can't press the bottle in, it's ready to be opened slowly.

QUIZ QUESTION:

WHAT WILL MAKE THE FIZZ?

A) A CHEMICAL REACTION BETWEEN LEMON JUICE AND SUGAR

B) THE YEAST

C) MICROBES IN THE GINGER

ANSWER: B

FUNNEL

WHAT HAPPENS?

Yeasts are microscopic fungi. Unlike animals, yeasts can live without oxygen. They produce carbon dioxide gas as they turn sugar into alcohol. You can probably hear the gas fizzing during Step 3.

BOTTLE

WOODEN WONDERS

Can you see the wood for the trees?

NATURE EXPERIMENTS

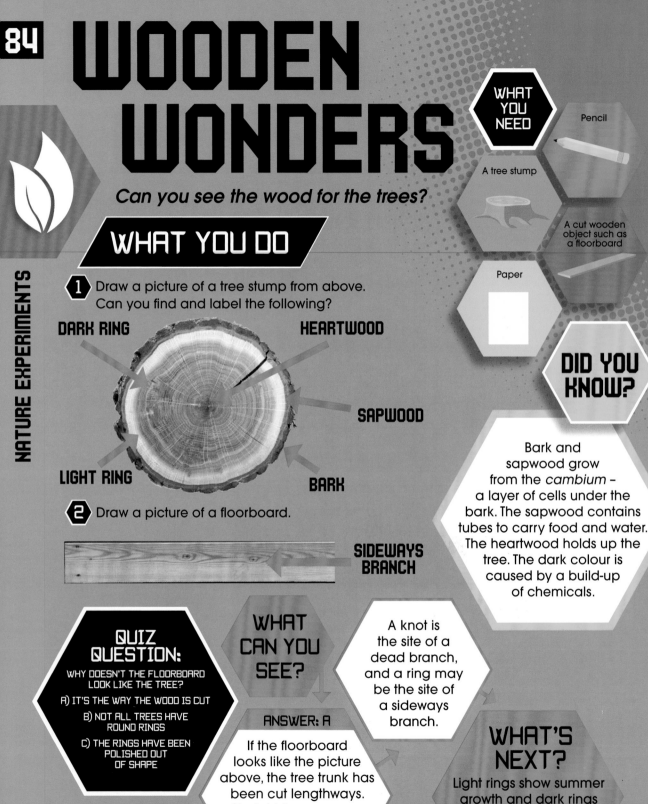

WHAT YOU DO

1 Draw a picture of a tree stump from above. Can you find and label the following?

DARK RING

HEARTWOOD

SAPWOOD

LIGHT RING

BARK

2 Draw a picture of a floorboard.

SIDEWAYS BRANCH

WHAT YOU NEED

Pencil

A tree stump

A cut wooden object such as a floorboard

Paper

DID YOU KNOW?

Bark and sapwood grow from the *cambium* – a layer of cells under the bark. The sapwood contains tubes to carry food and water. The heartwood holds up the tree. The dark colour is caused by a build-up of chemicals.

QUIZ QUESTION:

WHY DOESN'T THE FLOORBOARD LOOK LIKE THE TREE?

A) IT'S THE WAY THE WOOD IS CUT

B) NOT ALL TREES HAVE ROUND RINGS

C) THE RINGS HAVE BEEN POLISHED OUT OF SHAPE

WHAT CAN YOU SEE?

ANSWER: A

If the floorboard looks like the picture above, the tree trunk has been cut lengthways. Straight lines mean a straight cut, wavy lines means the saw cut through rings.

A knot is the site of a dead branch, and a ring may be the site of a sideways branch.

WHAT'S NEXT?

Light rings show summer growth and dark rings show winter growth. Why are summer rings wider than winter rings?

CRAZY SPROUT HAIR

Here's a really fun scientific experiment that will show you how to grow hair... on an egg!

WHAT YOU NEED

Cress seeds

Jug of water

Empty eggshells

Cotton wool

WHAT YOU DO

1. Draw funny faces on your eggshells.
2. Half fill the eggshells with cotton wool.
3. Place ten seeds on top of the cotton balls.
4. Pour a little water inside. Make sure the cotton wool is wet without being drenched.
5. Place one eggshell in a dark cupboard (eggshell 1) and one eggshell near a window with lots of light (eggshell 2).
6. Check on your eggshells every day for four days, giving a small amount of water if the cotton wool feel dry.
7. On day 5, check the progress of your cress.

QUIZ QUESTION:

WHAT WILL YOUR CRAZY HAIR LOOK LIKE?

A) EGGSHELL 1 IS PALE, TALL AND SPINDLY. EGGSHELL 2 IS GREEN AND BUSHY

B) EGGSHELL 1 IS EMPTY. EGGSHELL 2 HAS GROWN FLOWERS

C) THERE'S NO CRESS AT ALL – THE DOG ATE IT!

WHAT'S NEXT?

Which cress tastes better? The cress that grew in the light or the cress that grew in the dark?

WHAT HAPPENS?

ANSWER: A

Plants develop green pigment in their leaves to make food using energy from sunlight. The cress in eggshell 1 is tall and spindly as it was seeking light. The cress in eggshell 2 is green, short and sturdy. It had light, so it developed the green pigment.

NATURE EXPERIMENTS

EGGSHELL 1

EGGSHELL 2

MAKE A BIRD FEEDER

Feeding birds is good for them and good for science too.

NATURE EXPERIMENTS

WHAT YOU DO

1 Ask an adult to cut an oval hole in the side of the bottle, large enough for a small bird (about 5 cm). Below this they should make holes for the pencil to poke through the bottle as shown. Add the pencil and use the funnel to pour 2-3 cm of birdseed into the bottle.

2 Ask the adult to make a few small holes in the bottle base to allow any rain to escape. The holes can't be too large or the seeds will fall out.

3 Tie the feeder to a washing line or tree branch that's visible from your home.

WHAT YOU NEED

Strong string

Birdseed

Plastic bottle

Pencil

Funnel

Scissors

QUIZ QUESTION:

WHY DO YOU NEED TO HANG THE BIRD FEEDER UP?

A) TO STOP CATS FROM EATING THE BIRDS

B) TO STOP OTHER ANIMALS FROM EATING THE FOOD

C) BOTH OF THESE

WHAT HAPPENS?

ANSWER: C

The feeder is designed for small seed-eating birds. Hanging the feeder makes it harder for squirrels and rats to steal food and harder for cats to ambush the feeding birds.

WHAT'S NEXT?

Use a bird book to identify the feeding birds. Do they feed at a particular time? What happens when two birds want to feed?

BOTTLE

SEEDS

PENCIL

BUG HUNT!

If you're a bug, it pays to be good at hiding.

WHAT YOU NEED

Pencil

Friend

Stopwatch

Coloured pencils

Paper

Small area of garden or an indoor room with lots of green and brown colours

WHAT YOU DO

1 You and your friend should each trace or photocopy six copies of the bug shape below.

2 Colour two bugs green, two brown, one red and give one yellow and black stripes.

3 Give the green and brown bugs matching, but not identical backgrounds. The colourful bugs can have green or brown backgrounds. Fold each bug lengthways so it stands up. Write your name on the back of your bugs.

4 Take turns hiding your bugs in the garden. You have five minutes to find each other's bugs.

NATURE EXPERIMENTS

QUIZ QUESTION:

WHAT WILL YOU FIND?

A) COLOURFUL BUGS ARE HARDEST TO FIND

B) BROWN BUGS ARE HARDER TO FIND THAN THE OTHER COLOURS

C) BUGS ARE HARDER TO FIND IF THEY'RE THE SAME COLOUR AS THEIR BACKGROUND

Brightly-coloured bugs are warning other creatures not to eat them. Red ladybirds taste bad and yellow and black wasps have nasty stings.

WHAT HAPPENS?

ANSWER: C

Some bugs are the same colour as the places they live in. This makes them harder to find. This type of colouring is known as *camouflage.*

DID YOU KNOW?

HOW TO TEST A WOODLOUSE

Now you can find out exactly how clever woodlice really are.

WHAT YOU DO

1 Place the jar on one side of the box. The jar should be 2 cm from the top surface. Draw around the jar. Ask an adult to partly cut around the jar's outline, leaving a flap that should be pulled out as shown below.

2 Tape the flaps at the top of the box and then place the box upside-down.

3 Place the woodlouse in the jar and put clingflim over the open top. Replace the jar in the box with the clingfilm-covered end sticking out at a slight angle. Make sure the side of the jar is facing a window. Watch what the woodlouse does.

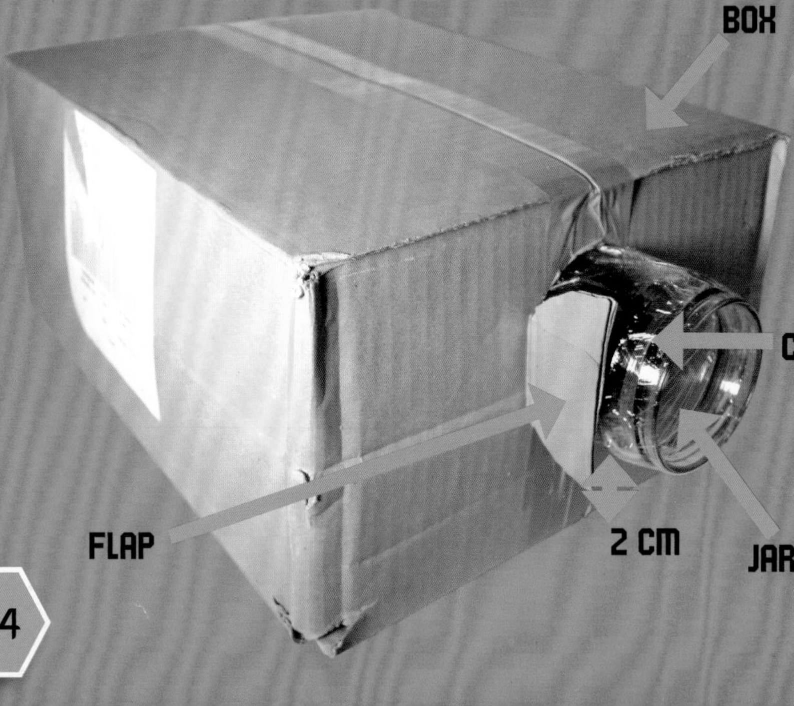

QUIZ QUESTION:

WHAT WILL THE WOODLOUSE DO?

A) IT WALKS IN CIRCLES

B) IT WALKS DOWN TO THE DARK AREA

C) IT STAYS WHERE IT IS

WHAT HAPPENS?

ANSWER: B

Woodlice normally live in dark places, where they can find shelter and food. It's not surprising that the woodlouse prefers the darker area, even though it has to climb down the slippery glass slope to reach it.

BOX

CLINGFILM

FLAP

2 CM

JAR

NATURE EXPERIMENTS

DID YOU KNOW?

There are 5,000 **species** of woodlouse. They're not insects, though. In fact, they're related to crabs and lobsters. They mostly eat dead plant material. Larger creatures rarely eat woodlice because it's hard to bite through their armoured coats and they taste horrible!

Woodlice prefer damp places. That's why they go towards the cotton wool.

WHAT'S NEXT?

Repeat the experiment with damp cotton wool at the far end of the jar. Place the experiment in a cool, dark place. After an hour, look for the woodlouse. Which end does it prefer this time? Why is this?

WHAT YOU NEED

Pencil

Woodlouse

Sticky Tape

Cardboard box with lid or flaps

Glass jar

Scissors

Clingfilm

Coton wool

NATURE QUIZ

ADD THE MISSING WORDS:

1) YEASTS ARE MICROSCOPIC F____.

2) C_____ IS A LAYER OF CELLS FOUND UNDER TREE BARK.

3) A CHAMELEON USES ITS LONG T_____ TO CATCH INSECTS.

Answers: 1) Fungi, 2) Cambium, 3) Tongue.

THE MYSTERY EXPERIMENT

Can YOU make sense of this science surprise?

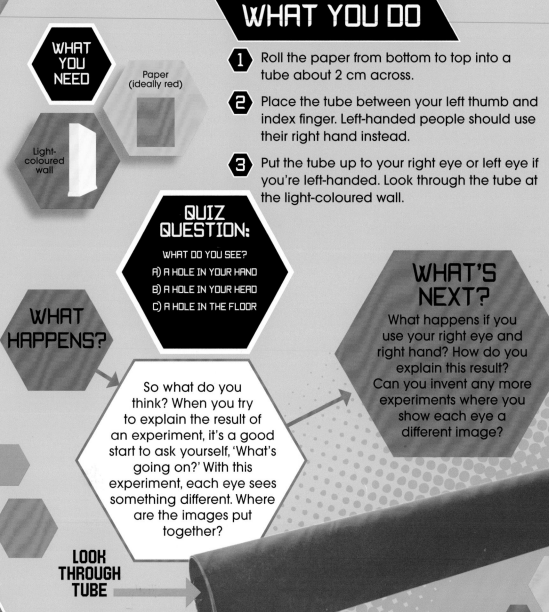

WHAT YOU NEED

Paper (ideally red)

Light-coloured wall

WHAT YOU DO

1 Roll the paper from bottom to top into a tube about 2 cm across.

2 Place the tube between your left thumb and index finger. Left-handed people should use their right hand instead.

3 Put the tube up to your right eye or left eye if you're left-handed. Look through the tube at the light-coloured wall.

QUIZ QUESTION:

WHAT DO YOU SEE?

A) A HOLE IN YOUR HAND

B) A HOLE IN YOUR HEAD

C) A HOLE IN THE FLOOR

WHAT'S NEXT?

What happens if you use your right eye and right hand? How do you explain this result? Can you invent any more experiments where you show each eye a different image?

WHAT HAPPENS?

So what do you think? When you try to explain the result of an experiment, it's a good start to ask yourself, 'What's going on?' With this experiment, each eye sees something different. Where are the images put together?

LOOK THROUGH TUBE

116

For the answer, turn to page 120!

GLOSSARY

Air pressure
The force of the air pressing on something. Air pressure increases with temperature.

Air resistance
A form of friction or slowing force caused by air acting on a moving object.

Atom
A particle made up of a nucleus (containing protons and neutrons), usually surrounded by electrons. It's hard to break atoms into smaller particles.

Cell
Living unit that makes up larger life-forms. Cells can divide to make more cells.

Cellulose fiber
Fibres formed from cellulose – a polymer found in plants and trees.

Charge
Charged objects can attract and repel each other. Inside atoms, electrons have negative charge and protons have positive charge.

Density
The mass of a certain volume of a substance.

Dissolved
When a solid breaks into smaller particles in a liquid, such as water.

Friction
The force that occurs when two surfaces pass over each other.

Gravity
The force that pulls every object with mass together. On Earth, it pulls objects towards the planet's centre.

Inertia
The quality that keeps an object motionless or moving in a straight line unless another force affects it.

Indicator
Substances that change colour when they are added to acidic or alkaline solutions.

Ions
An atom or molecule that has become electrically charged after losing or gaining electrons.

Light waves
Light waves are both electric and magnetic. They travel in a straight line. The colour we see depends on the length of the waves.

Mass
The matter (atoms, etc.) that makes up an object.

Molecule
A group of atoms joined together. They can form or break up in chemical reactions.

Photosynthesis
The way green plants make sugar from carbon dioxide and water using energy from light.

Polymers
Molecule formed from lots of smaller molecules arranged in a chain.

Radiation
A form of energy given out by atoms. It could be electromagnetic radiation, such as light waves.

Reflect
When light, heat or sound bounces off a surface without being absorbed by it.

Species
A group of animals or other living things that normally breed together.

Surface tension
Surfaces of liquids such as water are springy because the molecules are slightly drawn together.

INDEX

PICTURE CREDITS

MYSTERY EXPERIMENT ANSWER

Close your right eye and you see your
left hand in front of your left eye. Switch eyes
and you see the bright circle at the end of the
tube in the same place as you saw your hand.
When you look with both eyes together, your
brain mixes (superimposes) the two
images and you see the bright circle
in the middle of your hand. The
circle is much brighter than
your hand, so you
only see the circle.